DEDICATION

To Ali and my beautiful girls, Amy and Bunny.
May your 'fiddle fingers' lead the way one day!
xXx

Appliqué Art

ABIGAIL MILL

SEARCH PRESS

First published in 2014

Search Press Limited
Wellwood, North Farm Road,
Tunbridge Wells, Kent TN2 3DR

Text copyright © Abigail Mill 2014

www.abigailmill.co.uk

Photographs by Paul Bricknell

Photographs and design copyright © Search Press Ltd 2014

ISBN: 978-1-84448-868-1

The Publishers and author can accept no responsibility for any
consequences arising from the information, advice or instructions
given in this publication.

Suppliers
For details of suppliers, please visit the Search Press website:
www.searchpress.com

Printed in China

ACKNOWLEDGEMENTS

I would like to say a big thank you to my parents for passing
down their artistic genes, for never stifling my creativity and
for always being supportive of my freelance career.
My family have been very patient with me while I travel the
country exhibiting at various shows, leaving them to pick up
the pieces 'backstage' on the school run!
Huge thanks to Search Press for all of their enthusiasm
when putting this book together, and for making the
photoshoot so fun. Big thanks to Becky Shackleton and
Katie French for watching my every move during the
photoshoot to document all of the projects, and to
Paul Bricknell for keeping it so jolly, even when
shooting white on white!
The projects have sometimes been a challenge for me:
it has been a bit like teaching someone else to drive, as
it's difficult to break down something that you do so
automatically. It has been a hugely rewarding process
though and so lovely to see my images in print. I hope that
this book will be an inspiration to others to dust off their
sewing machines and try something new!

Publishers' note
All the step-by-step photographs in this book feature
the author, Abigail Mill. No models have been used.

Contents

Introduction

Since leaving art school over twenty years ago I have been really lucky to have converted my passion for embroidery into a career. Every time I exhibit I am reminded of this by appreciative collectors who are only able to find time to follow embroidery as a hobby. As a child I was nick-named 'fiddle-fingers' because I was always making, sewing, painting and could never sit still! My father, who worked in the film industry, used to come home at weekends with an array of colourful camera tape. This was one of the first artist's materials at my fingertips, and fuelled my creative instincts as I transformed it into miniature creatures.

As I grew up, the obvious path for me was a creative career and it was while I was at art school that I discovered textiles as a means of incorporating texture and colour with the three-dimensional qualities of fabric. I specialised in freehand machine embroidery, millinery and felt making. I soon discovered that machine embroidery was a transferable skill with no boundaries: from embroidering thick handmade felt jewellery and constructing felt embroidered hats, to playing with colour through fabric dyeing. It took time and patience – along with a few broken machine needles, the odd burnt-out sewing machine and a dye-splattered kitchen – but I gradually honed my craft. By the time I left, I was fortunate enough to have my first exhibition lined up and set up my studio soon after, with the help of a business development loan from the Prince's Trust.

Over years of experimentation, I have developed my own distinctive embroidery technique, my 'appliqué art'. I use layers of sheer fabric to build up the background design, adding further layers for depth of colour and texture. Over-dyed cottons are then added to create the foreground. I create texture using frayed and ruffled edges but I do not like to use straight lines, seams or hems. The pieces are then embellished with motif details, often padded with wadding, and defined with areas of freehand machine embroidery. Using this technique gives the embroidery an ethereal, watery feel; my artworks are often confused with watercolour paintings from a distance. The images are inspired by my native Norfolk and Suffolk coastlines, as well as country cottage gardens, which conjure up a feeling of nostalgia.

When I was first approached by Search Press to write this book, I was a busy mum juggling work with young children and the timing just wasn't right. But ten years later, spurred on by the level of public interest in textiles and the resurgence of craft in general, it was a different matter. So here it is! A collection of techniques and projects to inspire you to have a go yourself. Just remember… practice makes perfect! Freehand machine embroidery is all about you leading the machine and it is an organic process. It may not go entirely the way that you envisaged, but go with it and see what you create. Remember to leave all of your edges raw and frayed for texture, and no straight lines!

Abigail Mill

Split Screen Ice Cream

55 x 55cm (22 x 22in)

I was at a craft fair in Henley, Oxfordshire, when I came across this 1969 split screen Volkswagen ice cream van. There were only five ever made, and I was inspired to try and replicate it in embroidery. I got carried away with the detail, trying to capture the essence of the van in an English fête scenario.

Materials and equipment

If you have an interest in craft and sewing you will probably already have an array of fabrics in your collection, along with threads and trimmings. I have met many people who quilt and are interested in learning how to freehand machine embroider in order to use up all of their little scraps and leftovers. They will have most of the materials that they need to hand already without having to spend a fortune. If you do need a supply of fabric, why not try riffling through some charity shops with an eye to finding fabrics that you can work with and upcycle. While you are looking through the racks think about the fabric weights, colours and patterns. The possibilities are endless and it is how you put together your colourways, ideas and inspiration that will make your work unique.

I would advise using a sewing machine, and you will need one that can be converted to freehand embroidery on a darning setting. For the stitching you will need regular sewing cotton but other machine embroidery threads can add some extra texture and interest in places. Next on the 'Essential List' are pins, sharp fabric scissors, embroidery hoops and a tape measure. I would also recommended investing in some craft or fabric glue. This is one of my all-time 'Top Tips', as it is useful for attaching together tiny pieces of fabric that will need to be appliquéd without excessive pinning – if the glue is used in a small amount it won't show and bleed through the fabric. Another good investment is a water-soluble pen, which can be used for marking out lines or areas of stitching and as a guide for lettering before you sew.

Once the work is finished, you will need a large piece of mountboard to stretch the embroidery on, although your local framing shop should be able to do this for you.

Fabrics

Like anyone with a love for textiles, nothing excites me more than discovering a new fabric and being inspired by its potential. My own collection, which has grown considerably over the last twenty years, takes up a lot of space. I have fabrics stored in favourite colours, patterns, fabric types, and sizes but unbelievably I often don't have quite the right piece and have to go fabric shopping again. I source my fabric from many places – it is easy these days to buy exciting fabrics, either in your local haberdashery shop, major department stores, Asian fabric shops or on the internet. Most fabric shops are willing to cut small amounts so you don't have to spend a fortune to start off your collection. When choosing fabric, think about the project that you have in mind and select the colours, patterns and textures accordingly. For example, if you are creating a seaside scene, choose a range of sheer blues and greens for the sea and sky and yellows and browns for the sand.

Colour

I am a big fan of over-dyeing printed cottons to create my own personal colour range. This might seem like a lot of extra work but I use a simple hot water dye. See pages 22–23 for guidance and tips. As you can see from the image left, dyeing creates a wonderful range of effects on different fabrics, and can help tone fabrics together for an image.

Organzas

The background fabric that I tend to use is polyester organza – I start each picture with a white base and then layer it with coloured pieces. Although a sheer fabric, it is very sturdy when stretched in a hoop and will withstand the weight of the embroidery. I also use small dark pieces of organza to shade my appliqué and give the feeling of depth, such as the horizon line on page 31 or the trees in the Hen House project on pages 96–103.

Cottons

Patterned patchwork fabric is brilliant for building up colour and texture within an image and is ideal for over-dyeing. There is an incredible range of colours and patterns available, including many that feature pictures of items you might want to incorporate, such as the strawberry print that has been cut out and used on page 61, and the ice cream print cotton used on page 47.

Lamé

Only to be used in small quantities as it is quite difficult to integrate, lamé can be great for creating shimmering water and metallic effects when overlaid with organza – see the Cakestand and Sugar Bowl project on pages 68–75 and the headlights on the Ice Cream Van on page 7.

Threads

For the top thread I work with good-quality silk machine embroidery threads. I use regular cotton for the bobbin thread, as it is more economical, unless I'm pulling it through and want the colour to show (see pages 26 and 27). Choose a good-quality metallic thread – if you find that it keeps snapping, change the needle to a larger size and loosen the tension. Sometimes metallic threads can dry out if you've had them a while, so spin off the top layer and try again. The main thing to remember about embroidery threads is that you can never have enough colours! I have a massive collection because colour is really important to me and, like an artist picking out a paint colour, I like to have a good selection to hand to choose from.

Wadding

I often like to raise areas or motifs with wadding to make my work more three-dimensional. You can easily alter the depth and shape of wadding to fit your embroidery by pulling away the fibres to create a soft shape, or cutting it with scissors to create a harder edge. Wadding can be secured underneath fabric and machined through or hand sewn onto the back of a motif and moulded into shape.

Trims and embellishments

If you are anything like me, you might already have a selection of treasures tucked away that are great for embellishing your embroidery with those all important 'finishing touches'. Start collecting buttons, beads, ribbons and lace so that you have a good range of coordinating colours to choose from.

Embroidery hoop

I would recommend using an embroidery hoop for freehand machining. Because this type of sewing requires you to take the tension out of the machine, you will need to compensate with the fabric and stretch it as tight as a drum. If you don't, you will have problems with your thread tension. There are many sizes of hoops available, so choose a hoop that sits inside your fabric edge but is larger than the piece that you are working on. Make sure that you have space to turn the hoop under the machine. If your embroidery is large then you can keep moving the hoop to fit the area that you are working on. Lay your fabric out on a flat surface and loosen off the tension screw before you line up the hoop top and bottom. There is no need to over tighten the hoop as this will mark, and can sometimes tear a sheer fabric. Push the inside hoop 2mm (1/16in) lower than the outside one to stop the hoop catching on the machine bed (see page 32).

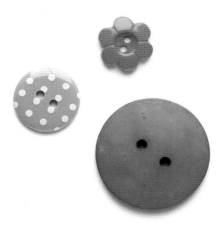

Sewing machine

If you are a keen embroiderer or crafter you may well have a trusty sewing machine already – the great thing about freehand machine embroidery is that you will need very little new sewing equipment and you should be able to use your existing machine. If you don't already have a machine and are looking to invest, a basic machine with straight stitch is perfectly adequate.

The main difference from standard machining is the tension on the machine. To convert your normal sewing machine for freehand embroidery you need to check that the feed dogs on the bottom of the machine can drop down. This can be done by either using the darning setting, or by screwing on a plate over the top of the feed dogs. The other change that you will need to make is to use a darning foot. Some free-handers don't use a foot at all, but I wouldn't recommend this as it's a bit hazardous leaving your fingers exposed to a moving machine needle! Your machine will now be ready for freehand and it will be up to you to control the machine, rather than it controlling you. You may find it strange sewing without the feed dogs at first, but this technique is like drawing in stitching, and is where the fun begins!

Bobbins

As with embroidery threads, I find it really useful to have a good quantity of bobbins so that I have a large colour range to choose from. I pre-wind them ready to use before I start to embroider as rethreading to change the colour can take time.

Bobbincase

Once you've got the feel for freehand embroidery there are many techniques that you can experiment with through stitching. One technique is to loosen off the bobbin thread so that it is pulled through to the top of the embroidery, creating loops and textures. This can be great fun, especially if you contrast the colours of the top and bottom threads (see pages 26 and 27). If you can afford to have a separate bobbincase on the go for experimentation then do so. Once you start altering the bobbin tension it can be hard to reset it, which may be problematic if you also want to do dress-making or other more precise stitching.

Needles

Needles play a crucial role in alleviating the tension problems that freehand can cause. I would recommend buying good-quality needles that are highly polished. A cheaper needle eye can shred metallic threads, and a quality sharp point will really help cut through the fabric. I mainly use a medium size needle, either 80 or 90, as I work with a lot of sheer fabrics, but I would recommend 100 for thick fabric to give your machine a helping hand!

Scissors

Scissors are some of my most important tools. I use two types of scissors: a large heavy-duty pair for cutting lengths of fabric, and smaller embroidery scissors for cutting out more precise details. In order to keep them sharp, your scissors should *only* be used to cut fabric – they should not be used on paper. I have built up a collection over the years and I have them numbered in order so that I can keep my newest sharpest ones for best!

Other useful tools

Dress-making marker pens are great if you are nervous about freehand machining lettering or small, precise details – simply draw in the lines, sew over and then remove them (see page 59). The pens are available as water soluble or light reactive. Another fantastic tool is a glue stick, as this will allow you to join together tiny pieces of fabric without the need for excessive pinning. The fabric pieces can be readjusted if you don't get the arrangement right the first time, and the glue won't seep through to the front of the fabric. You will also need pins and needles, a tape measure and white card or mountboard for mounting your finished pictures.

Inspiration

Before you start to think that I am a floaty artist drifting around with my sketchbook documenting daily pieces of inspiration, let me tell you that unfortunately that is a long way from the truth! Due to everyday time pressures, if I spot a scene or object that I think will work well as an image, I will often just snap pictures on my smartphone while I am out and about and then print them off at home. When I do have a bit more time, I find that a quick pencil sketch is enough to jog my memory later, as the rest of the composition comes naturally during the construction of the embroidery. Sometimes, however, I am inspired by something as simple as the bundles of fabric on my workbench. The possibilities are endless, but unfortunately time is not.

However, the initial idea is not always the end of the story. I will often have an image, or elements of an image, brewing in my head that could take up to a year to come to life; I also tend to work through themes – with one picture leading to the next using a similar subject matter. Up until the point when I am actually cutting and pinning the layers of the design, I have scope to change the composition, but once it is stitched, that's it! If I make a mistake I have found it is quicker to work over it, than to unpick it and try again.

Inspired by my native Suffolk and countless beach walks, I have tried to capture the horizon of the sea against the brightly coloured and eclectic beach huts. The piece features several raised, padded areas, such as the parasol, ball and ice cream sign.

Seaside

I went to school in Southwold, Suffolk – the seaside was never far away and is the scene of many of my earliest memories, such as invigorating coastal walks at weekends, which usually finished in a pub! During my favourite walk from Southwold harbour to Walberswick I have been lucky enough to see seals bobbing around in the harbour and I just love the contrast of the black fisherman's shacks against the sandy shoreline and muddy banks, with the boats nearby in the water. The seaside is still a huge inspiration to me, and one closest to my heart. It is the easiest subject matter for me to work with and my watery style and colour palette suit the imagery. There are elements of seaside scenes that crop up in several of my pieces, such as seals and beach huts. Always remember that if you find elements that you like or that are dear to you, there is no reason why you can't use them time and again as signature motifs.

Make sketches on location if you can, and take inspiration from found objects such as shells and driftwood, family photographs and the colours and styles found in nautical fabrics.

17

Gardens

With your camera or sketchbook to hand, go out into your garden or take a walk through the countryside. Try to capture large subjects as well as details: I can become obsessed with the smallest detail, such as the stonework on the side of a Norfolk cottage. It may seem like a lot of information, but this detail can help to inform your stitching or fabric choices later on and will breathe life into your pictures. If you are interested in creating floral pictures, consider visiting a flower show. In the UK I exhibit at a lot of Royal Horticultural Society events and, with smartphone in hand, it is pretty easy to capture inspiring and useful images. The only thing that I can't recreate from a floral marquee are the amazing fragrances! The density of colours and the delicacy of the floral displays can be amazing – I use photographs of flowers as reference for floral foreground details.

Fruits and vegetables also make great subjects for pictures, such as those on display at the old Cley Forge (see pages 48–49). Take close-ups of any elements that jump out at you, but remember that a photograph is just inspirational and can be adapted if necessary to suit your design. Use this artistic licence when choosing floral fabrics for your garden scenes: creating layers of flowerbeds using printed cottons can be an effective way to enrich a scene, see right.

Take photographs of eye–catching flowers, fruits and vegetables, make sketches of houses, gardens and flowerbeds, and collect floral and fruity fabrics.

Country Cottage

56 x 56cm (22 x 22in)

This country cottage embroidery is often described as a 'dream cottage' – the house that many people would like to live in! For me, the most important features of this picture are the colourful layers of the flowerbeds, the three-dimensional roof and the rambling roses around the door.

Colour

Colour has always been a massive inspiration to me and it is an integral part of my work and life. I'd like to thank my parents at this stage for turning a blind eye to my rainbow-coloured hair in my teenage years! The choice of fabric colour is a crucial element of my work. Whether creating a sea scene in blue hues and shimmery fabrics or a picture of an English garden with rich greens and printed cotton florals, it is essential to get the colours right. I look to contrast colours and incorporate bright rich accents, like bright stripy beach huts and pink floral flowerbeds. I tend to mix 'off the peg' fabrics with fabrics that I over-dye myself. These cottons are patterned patchwork fabrics, mostly with a floral print design on a small scale. If you dye your own fabric it opens up a larger colour spectrum to choose from, which will be more inspiring to embroider and easier to integrate naturally within a picture. Of course, it is then important to contrast or complement these fabrics with bright, beautiful stitching.

Shading with a colour is also possible, by placing strips of fabric next to each other that gradually darken or lighten in tone. You can also introduce strips of dark organza layered over base fabrics to give the feeling of depth and tone (see below). You could use this effect on the edge of a beach hut, along the base of a boat, or running along the edge of a tea stand. Shimmery or lamé fabrics can also be used, but I only tend to use them sparingly. As effective as they can be, there is nothing worse that a piece of appliqué that looks 'stuck on' rather than being easy on the eye. For that same reason I also avoid using black, unless I really need to emphasise a deep tone.

Layering organzas over coloured cottons can give a real intensity of colour and creates a beautifully soft effect.

When composing your pictures, play around with contrasting, brightly coloured fabrics and threads – sometimes the most unexpected pattern and colour combinations look striking together.

Over–dyeing your fabrics

Over-dyeing is a simple process that allows you to create unique and unusual fabrics for your projects. It is a handy trick to have up your sleeve, especially if the detail of a fabric is perfect for a project you're working on, but the background colour is not quite right; the idea of over-dyeing is to give a hint of a colour, while still letting the original pattern show through. Once you are confident with the dyeing process you might want to experiment with the effects you can create. For a marbled effect that is useful for shading, twist the fabric and secure it before you place it in the dye, or try tie-dyeing, dip-dyeing, or using fabrics with different textures – the dye will take differently to each. Trial and error can produce some beautiful effects – even if you weren't intending them – so play around with fabrics, dye colours and mixing time. In this example I have used a blue dye on a range of floral cotton patchwork fabrics with pale or white backgrounds – the aim is to create a range of blue-toned fabrics that will work well together.

1 Following the manufacturer's instructions, place the necessary amount of dye powder in a jam jar or similar container. Add the corresponding amount of hot water, and stir thoroughly until the powder is completely dissolved. The dyes can be an irritant, so wear rubber gloves to protect your hands.

2 Whether you are using hot-water dye and mixing the dye over heat, or using cold-water dye, the basic process is the same. Pour the concentrated dye mix into a large, sturdy container – an old jam pan is ideal – and stir it thoroughly again.

3 Household salt is needed to fix the dye and ensure that it won't run from the fabric if you ever wash it or get it wet. Follow the manufacturer's instructions and add the correct amount of salt into your dye mix – some dyes require you to dissolve the salt before adding, and others provide a dye-fix solution as well. Stir thoroughly.

4 Rinse your fabrics to remove any starch – this will enable them to absorb the dye properly. Add the fabrics to the dye mix one by one and stir until they are completely covered. The longer you leave in a fabric, the deeper the colour will be; keep checking the depth of the colour by pulling the fabric out.

5 Once you are happy with your colour, remove the fabrics from the dye mix and rinse them with cold water until the water runs clear. Hang them up to dry naturally or iron them dry when they are slightly damp – use protective cloths when doing so to protect your iron and ironing board. Don't be afraid to experiment with dyeing – it is easy to create lots of different wonderful colours and effects from just one dye pot.

Texture

Texture is a crucial element of my artworks. I start by cutting lengths of my favourite patterned cottons and fray all the edges – bear in mind that some fabrics will fray more easily than others. I build up the strips of fabric in the foreground, layering up individual pieces and ruffling them as I go. These ruffled pieces are then secured with embroidery. This can be hugely effective for a soft look, creating flowerbeds in garden pieces, waves in sea scenes, and sand dunes on beaches (see below, left). I have had a few comments from patchworkers that I 'don't finish off my edges' but for me that is the whole point! Freehand should be free and so should the way that you treat your fabric: it is about the overall creative effect.

It is also worth experimenting with stitching, as freehand machine embroidery can create some fantastic textural effects. There are so many ways to do this but the best approach is trial and error. Try solid stitching over and over to build up grassy areas; vary the machine speed to increase the density of stitches, or make them really long by moving the hoop faster. Long stitches can also be cut and frayed.

Appliqué

The term 'appliqué' literally means 'to add' and that is exactly what you do. Cut out shapes and motifs and add these as another layer at the end stages of the embroidery to create extra surface texture. These pieces can be key elements in the design and need to be sewn around to hold them down. I like to use a darker tone thread to define the shape, like a red around a beach ball or dark grey around a seal, see below. If you want to create a three-dimensional piece, trap wadding underneath for a chunkier look.

Build up layers of ruffled, frayed fabric to create a soft, ethereal look.

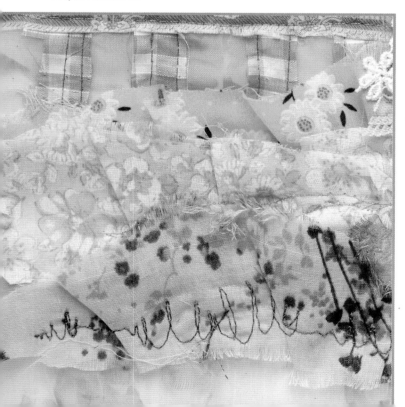

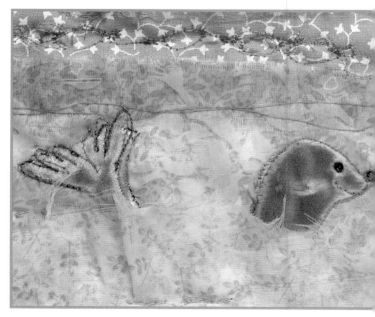

Outline your appliqué shapes with dark stitching – use more than one colour for extra definition, as with the seal's tail.

Pattern

Working with patterned fabric can look really effective – if you get the patterns right, it can be a quick and attractive way of building up the elements of an embroidery. Think about your fabric design: blue and white stripes are ideal for a deckchair, red and white stripes for a beach hut, and florals for a garden. Watch the scale of a pattern, too – it can be difficult to integrate large-sized prints in an embroidery, so use them sensitively. I have some favourite pieces of patterned fabric that are absolute treasures to me and probably irreplaceable once they are used up, but they just work with everything, so keep your eyes peeled for versatile, interesting patterns, such as the foliage fabric used below.

Make sure that the scale of the pattern fits the object – these strawberries are the perfect size to fill this wheelbarrow.

Matching the pattern to the item you are representing adds a playful and attractive level of detail.

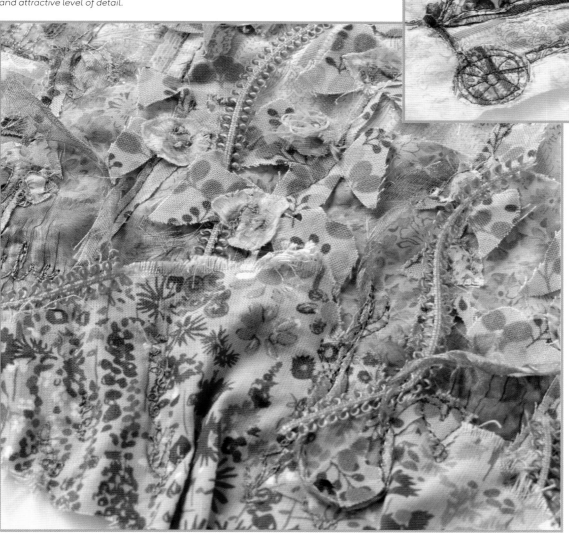

Stitching

Freehand machine stitching is a key design feature of my work – I think of it like drawing with a sewing machine. With some thought and imagination it can transform your picture into something really special, and it is easy to create some amazing effects – use the techniques listed here as a starting point and have a play around to find out what effects you like. Try to use the stitching to emphasise and highlight elements of your design – use complementary or contrasting thread colours to outline, define and draw or write in details.

I like to experiment with the tension on the bobbincase and loosen it off so that the bottom thread is pulled through by the top tension to create a loopy effect. Play around with thread colours – maybe use a light green on the bobbin and a dark green on the top. This works really well for grass and moss. Tightening the top tension exaggerates this look, which could be used for coral on a sea bed or pebbles on a beach.

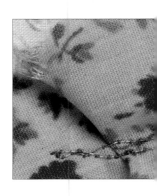

Outlining

Outline your motifs in contrasting or complementary colours to draw attention to the shapes. Outline even tiny details such as handles, lids and bottled sweets.

Special effects

Experiment with the thread tensions to create wonderful loopy effects – this can work really well on sheer fabrics, such as organzas, as the stitching is clearly visible.

Creating definition

You don't need to cut your fabric to the exact shape of your object every time – why not cut the piece roughly and let the stitching do the work? Choose a dark thread, such as the brown thread shown left, which will show up clearly against the fabric underneath.

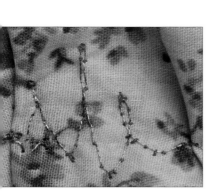

Thread colours

Mixing up the colours of your top and bobbin threads can create some beautiful effects if you loosen the bobbin tension so that its thread is pulled through to the surface.

Mimicking natural shapes

When attaching an object, such as a foreground ruffle (above, left) or an area of foliage (above, right), imitate its natural shapes: create tall, grass-like spikes for grass and sand dunes, swirling, curved shapes for tree tops, and curving stems lined with pointy leaf shapes for foliage.

Writing

Personalise your pictures with words, phrases and names. Use this technique sparingly and only pick out key elements, such as shop signs and boats.

Drawing

Use stitching as an element of your motifs – it works especially well for delicate, fine details such as the stream of golden tea flowing from the teapot above.

Building a scene

All the projects in this book contain the same basic elements: a layered organza and cotton background, motifs, padded shapes and the defining detail – the freehand machine embroidery. Many of the techniques used are the same from project to project, so you will quickly pick up skills that you can use throughout the book. In this project we will work through the steps in detail so that you can refer back to this section later on if you need to.

Preparing your organza backing

The base of this project – and every project in the book – is a square of white organza. To create the background you will layer plain and patterned blue organzas on top for the sky and green organzas for the beach. Every project starts in this way – you will select your organza pieces based on the colour of your scene, and cut and fray them before use to create extra texture.

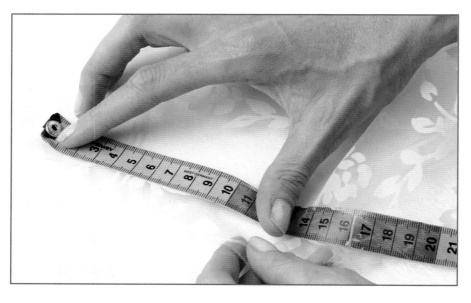

1 The base of this project is a square of white organza measuring 40 x 40cm (16 x 16in). You will also need to measure out some plain blue organza (30 x 25cm/ 12 x 10in), patterned blue organza (30 x 10cm/12 x 4in) and patterned green organza (30 x 15cm/12 x 6in). These are the sizes used in the example shown above, but you could make the organza pieces larger or smaller if you wanted to create a slightly different design.

2 Cut each of your organza pieces to size using sharp fabric scissors.

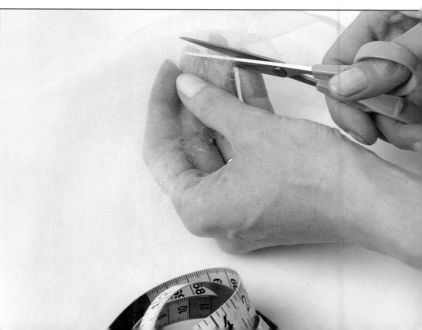

TIP

Always cut your white organza 5cm (2in) larger all round than the size you want your final piece to be, so that you have a large enough border for mounting.

3 Fray each of the edges of the blue patterned organza by stretching the fabric between your fingers and teasing the threads apart – this gives a lovely distressed effect.

4 Once all four edges are frayed, take sections of the fabric and tug them firmly apart to pucker and distort the organza.

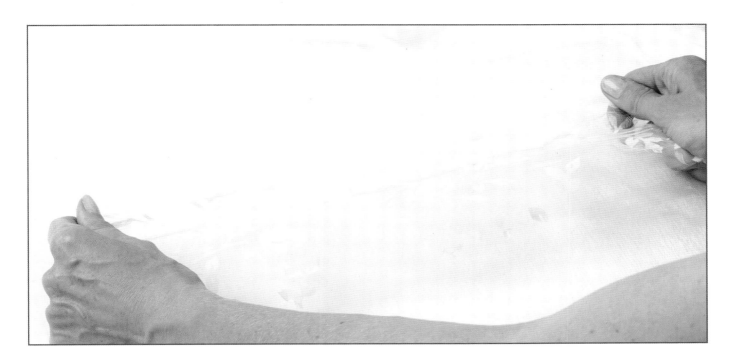

5 Hold the strip of organza out in front of you and, holding each end firmly, twist and stretch the fabric to create more puckers and texture. Stretch out the fabric so that it lies flat. Repeat steps 3–5 for the piece of patterned green organza.

6 Arrange your organzas on a flat, clean surface. Lay the white organza down first, then position the plain blue organza on top, centrally and 5cm (2in) down from the top edge. Lay the patterned green organza down next, placing it about 5cm (2in) from the bottom edge; its top edge will overlap the bottom of the plain blue. Finally, lay down the blue patterned organza about 5cm (2in) from the top of the plain blue organza. Pin the patterned green organza in place first, trapping all three layers of fabric.

7 Pin the patterned blue organza in place, securing all the layers as you do so. Put a pin in each corner of the strip. This will hold your backing layers in place until you stitch through them.

8 With your organzas prepared, think carefully about the other background fabrics you want to use and which colours and patterns will work well. To create the design shown on page 28 – and large on pages 46–47 – soft sea- and sand-coloured floral cottons were chosen to form the next layer of the background.

Adding the cotton fabrics

The next stage in the process is to add a layer of cotton background and foreground fabrics, which will create depth and texture in your picture. After fraying, you will layer them up and create ruffles in some to create a sense of perspective. When all your fabrics are pinned in place you will prepare the piece for sewing by stretching it in an embroidery hoop.

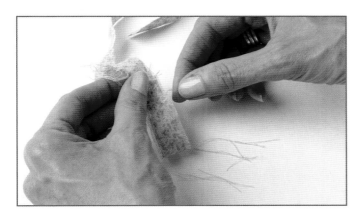

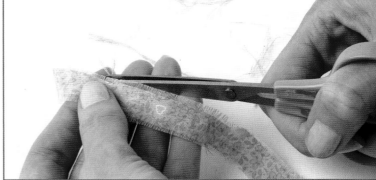

9 Here, four floral cottons were used: dark blue, mid-blue, pale blue and a sandy beige colour. Cut the fabric into strips, making them slightly longer than the 30cm (12in) width of the coloured organzas. Cut the dark blue 1.5cm (½in) tall, mid-blue 5cm (2in) tall, pale blue 10cm (4in) tall, and sandy beige 7cm (3in) tall. Make the shapes slightly irregular for a natural look. Fray the edges of each as you did for the organza in step 3.

10 Pull the loose threads out as you fray the edges – if they become too shaggy, trim them to leave a small fringe. It does not matter if the strips are not straight. Trim both ends of each to create triangular points.

11 Your colours should progress tonally from dark blue at the top through to sandy beige at the bottom. Place the darkest blue so that it sits about half way up the piece, just below the patterned blue organza. Layer the other strips on top, overlapping them slightly as you work down. You should still have a strip of patterned green organza visible at the bottom of the picture.

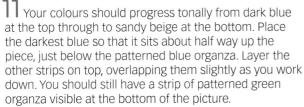

12 Remove any pins from the organza underneath the cotton strips. Once you are happy with your arrangement, pin the four strips in place, gathering the fabrics slightly along their length to create some extra texture; ensure that the pins go right through the organza layers as well. Cut a layer of dark blue organza 35cm (14in) wide and 2cm (¾in) tall, fray the edges and lay this over the dark blue cotton to create the horizon. Pin in place.

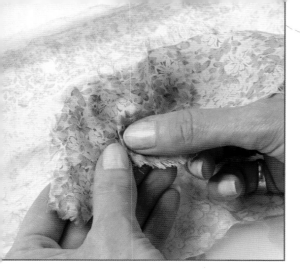

13 Take a piece of pale green floral cotton 20cm (8in) long and cut it so that it tapers from 5cm (2in) at one end to 2cm (¾in) at the other. Give the fabric a jagged outline – the aim is to create an organic looking shape. Fray the edges of the fabric as you did in steps 3 and 9. Gather the fabric between your fingers to create a slightly ruffled shape. This will form your foreground sand dune.

14 Pin the gathered sand dune shape into place at the bottom right of your picture. Pin it about 10cm (4in) from the right-hand edge of the white organza and with its upper edge slightly higher than the top of the sandy beige fabric.

15 Stretch the organza into a 30cm (12in) hoop. Lay the fabric over the outer hoop. Place the inner hoop on top and push it into the outer hoop, stretching the fabric between the two. Be careful not to catch any pins between the hoops.

16 Pull the fabric taut and tighten the hoop's screw if you need to. The inner hoop needs to sit slightly lower than the outer hoop.

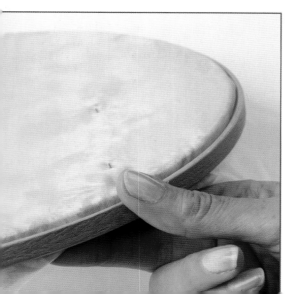

TIP

It is important to use an embroidery hoop when sewing as the shiny sheerness of the organza makes it a tricky fabric to work with – a hoop will keep it securely in place.

Stitching the background

With your fabric secured in your hoop it is time to think about sewing. All the projects in this book are sewn using freehand machine stitching. You will need to fit a darning foot on your machine and lower the feed dogs before you start. This method of sewing may take a little while to master, but it gives you the freedom to create exactly the shapes you want, from loose and flowing to tight and angular. The key to this kind of sewing is to try and match your stitch type to the subject you are sewing: it is easy to create lovely undulating waves or ripples in the sea, or to use a spiky, grass-like stitch to secure the foreground pieces. Colour is also crucial – think of your stitching as a feature of the piece: choose threads that contrast and complement your fabrics to bring the different elements to life. In most cases, you will either want to match your top thread and your bobbin thread or use colours that complement each other. The choice is yours, but I have noted throughout when I have chosen to use different top and bobbin colours in case you wish to do the same.

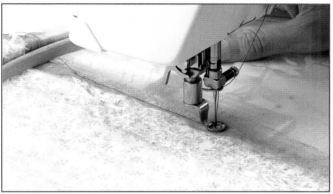

17 Set up your machine for freehand machine stitching by attaching a darning foot and lowering the feed dogs. With dark blue machine thread on top and a coordinating thread colour in your bobbin, sew along the strip of dark blue organza using straight stitch. The length of stitch is determined by how fast you move the hoop.

18 With turquoise cotton or silk thread in your machine, sew short lines of stitches, about 2–3cm (¾–1¼in) long, into the pale blue cotton background. Sew backwards and forwards to create thick, slightly wavy lines – sew over the first and last few stitches to secure the thread. Position the groups of stitches along two parallel lines, spacing them as shown.

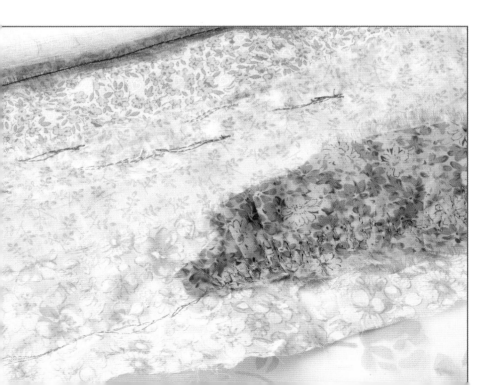

19 Using gold metallic thread sew several lines that curve gently back and forth across the sand, about 2.5cm (1in) from the bottom of the sandy beige cotton. Using lime green satin or silk thread, sew a zigzag of grass-like stitches along the bottom edge of the sand dune. Remove the pins that are no longer needed and trim all the thread ends.

Adding the main motifs

With your background complete, it's now time to think about the large motifs. Before you cut anything it's advisable to lay out all your fabrics and work out which you want to use – don't be afraid to jumble up patterns, colours and styles. I find that this often gives the best effect. As you are creating elements such as a wooden roof or slatted walls, try to find fabrics that reflect these, either in their colour or in their pattern, as this will help to bring your motifs to life. The templates for the more complex shapes are given below at the correct size – simple shape dimensions are given in the text – but if you are confident drawing freehand then simply cut out your motif shapes by eye – you can always adjust them if they are not quite right. The next stage will be to arrange the motifs on the background and sew them on.

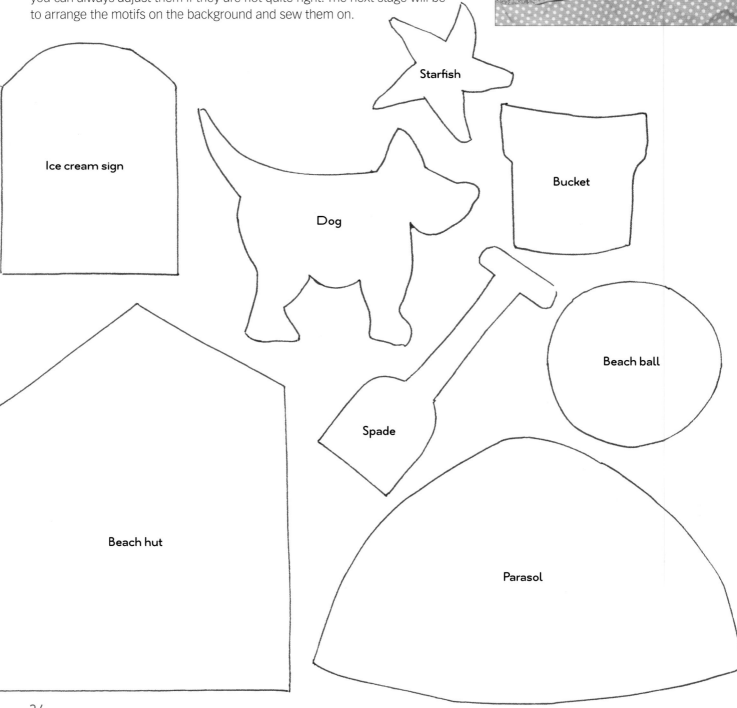

Ice cream sign

Starfish

Dog

Bucket

Spade

Beach ball

Beach hut

Parasol

20 Using the templates given left, create the pattern for the beach hut. You will need to create four beach huts in total – choose four or five coordinating fabrics for each. Pin the pattern to the fabric and cut round it using sharp scissors. Alternatively, cut out by eye.

21 You will need to create some additional pieces for each beach hut: the door should measure about 4 x 5cm (1½ x 2in), but adjust the size if you want it larger or smaller; the two roof pieces should each measure about 6 x 1½cm (2½ x ½in); the side panel should measure 10 x 1½cm (4 x ½in), with the top cut at angle, and you will also need a small triangle to form the flag on top, about 2cm (¾in) wide.

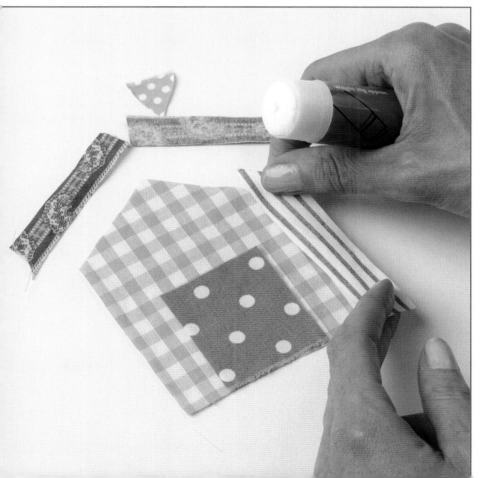

22 Use craft glue to lightly stick the pieces of the beach hut together. Attach the door, side panel and roof pieces. Glueing the pieces together makes it easy when you come to position the huts on the background; the pieces stay in place but can be pulled apart if you need to reposition or resize them.

23 Cut out and glue together the pieces for the other three beach huts. Choose a range of fabrics that will contrast well within the picture.

24 Cut strips of lace ribbon – here four different types have been used – slightly wider than the width of each beach hut. Glue the lace so that it sits snugly below the roof panels, tucking the ends of the lace under on each side.

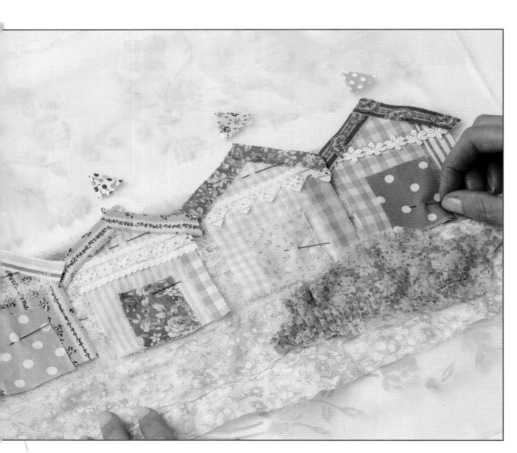

25 Remove the background from the hoop. Arrange the beach huts on the background; play around until you are happy with the layout and trim them down slightly, if you want to. Place them so that they sit at about the same level as the top of the sandy beige strip of background cotton. Pin them in place. Arrange the flags in position above – secure them with a spot of craft glue.

26 Place the fabric back in the embroidery hoop. Position the beach hut that you want to work on first in the centre of the hoop. Stretch the backing fabric until it is taut. Choose threads that will complement or contrast with the colours of your beach huts – the stitching is a feature, so choose your threads carefully as you want to be able to see the stitching.

27 Prepare your machine for freehand machine stitching; for this yellow beach hut I chose a lime green thread. Lift the corner of the right-hand roof panel and sew down the right side of the beach hut, trapping the lace in place as you go. Sew along the bottom of the beach hut as far as the door, sew up and around the inside of the door, then continue along the bottom of the hut and up the left-hand side; secure the other end of the lace as you do so, finishing your stitches underneath the left roof panel.

28 Sew on the door details: create a filled-in circle for the door knob and two elongated triangles for the hinges.

29 To attach the roof and the flag I changed to a brown machine thread. Start at the top edge of the left-hand side and follow the inverted 'v' shape three-quarters of the way round until you come to the middle of the lower edge. When you get to this point, create the flag pole by sewing straight up through the top of the 'v', trapping the flag in place as you do so. Sew back down the flag pole, then continue on around the 'v', to complete the roof.

30 Repeat this process for each of the huts, choosing whichever contrasting threads you want. Here, red, brown and pink threads were used on the pink tone beach huts, and dark blue was used on the blue beach hut. Trim off the threads once you have finished sewing.

Creating the padded motifs

With your large motifs in place it is time to add another layer of texture by creating a number of padded elements. The templates for all of these shapes are included on page 34, but pick and choose if you don't want to include them all. Again, select your fabrics carefully and try to match the colour or design to each motif. One of the padded motifs we will be making is an ice cream sign, for which the ice cream print fabric, shown right, is ideal. The motifs are all created on a piece of white organza stretched in an embroidery hoop, as this gives a taut surface on which to work. When the motifs are finished you will simply cut them out and sew them on, as any white organza left around the edges won't show against the background.

31 Using the template on page 34, create a paper pattern for the parasol top. Pin it to your fabric and cut around it using sharp fabric scissors. Position it so that the stripes run vertically down the parasol. Alternatively, if you are confident, cut out the shape by eye.

32 Create a pleat in the top of the shape and gather three folds of fabric together. Pin the folds in place. This creates a three-dimensional shape that, when padded out with wadding, will stand up from your background.

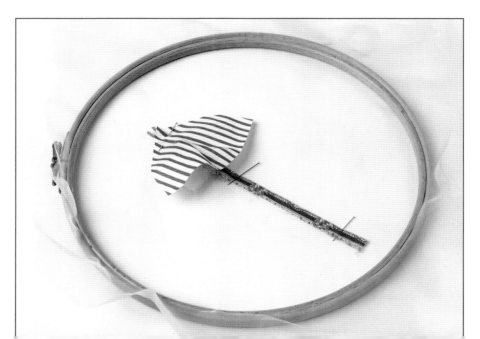

33 Stretch a piece of white organza taut in a 30cm (12in) embroidery hoop. Cut a strip of brown fabric, about 15 x 1cm (6 x ½in), and pin this down; this will form the pole for your parasol. Cut a piece of wadding the same shape as your parasol top but slightly smaller, and pin the wadding and the parasol top to the organza so that they appear to sit on top of the parasol pole – overlap the pole by about 2.5cm (1in) (see step 41 for reference).

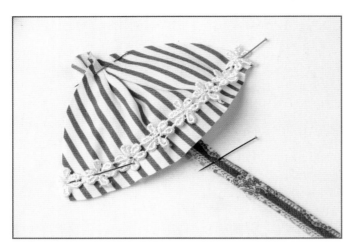

34 Cut a length of lace to the width of the parasol top and pin it in position around the lower edge. Ensure when you pin it that the skirt of the parasol is still slightly raised.

35 Using the template on page 34, cut out a beach ball shape. Cut a circle of wadding slightly smaller than this. Cut three evenly sized triangles from a contrasting fabric to form the ball stripes; round off their bottoms so that they fit neatly over the beach ball.

36 Attach the three rounded triangles to the beach ball shape with craft glue. Pin the beach ball onto the white organza on top of its circle of wadding.

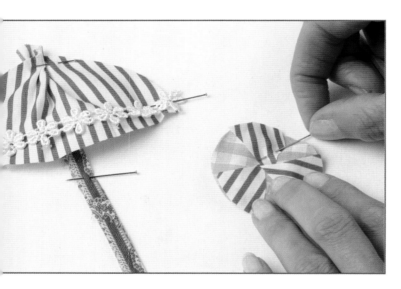

37 For the ice cream sign, use the template on page 34 and create two fabric shapes. Cut these out of contrasting fabrics – an ice cream print fabric is ideal if you can find it, then decide which piece you want on top and cut off the rounded top to create a rectangle. Cut a piece of wadding slightly smaller than the sign, and a piece of lace long enough to curve across the top and overhang the edges slightly. Pin these onto the organza as shown.

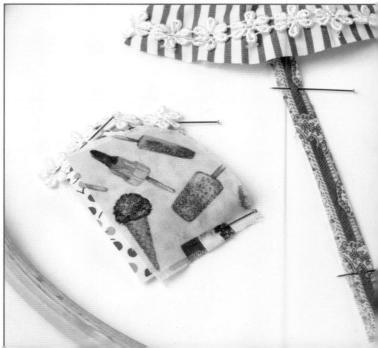

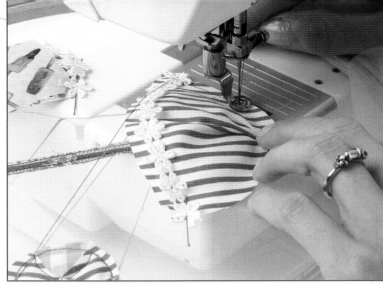

38 Stitch around the inside edge of the ball, a few mm in, and then around each triangle. Use a contrasting thread colour, such as the red top thread and pink bobbin thread used here, and remember that the stitching does not need to be perfect. There is no need to cut the threads each time – move on from one motif to the next. You will cut the threads in step 41.

39 Stitch the parasol pole in place by sewing down one side of it, across the bottom and up the other side – trap the wadding in place at the top as you do so. Secure the parasol top by sewing around the top of the curve, a few mm from the edge, sewing over the lace ends to hold it in place. Leave the bottom edge 'open' – do not sew around it.

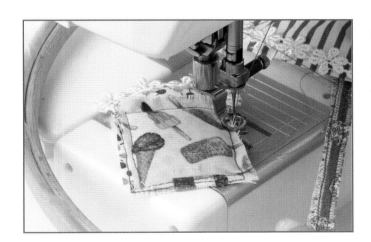

40 Sew a rectangle around the inside of your top layer of ice cream fabric, then go around the outer edge of the sign, securing the lace in place around the top edge as you go. Use the same red machine thread as you used for the parasol and the beach ball.

41 This view of the back of the organza shows what your stitching should look like. Once complete, cut away all your loose threads. Remove the organza from the hoop and cut out your motifs, cutting as close to the edge of the shapes as you can.

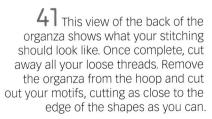

Adding the other elements

With your padded motifs completed, the final stages will be to prepare the rest of the motifs, sew everything in position and add any finishing touches – your piece will then be ready for mounting and framing. The key to making the piece look interesting is to create motifs from a variety of fabrics: the dog is made from paw print fleece, the bucket and spade from spotty cotton fabrics overlaid with organza, and the starfish is simply an organza shape decorated with stitching. As with your padded shapes, you will create your motifs on a piece of white organza stretched in an embroidery hoop.

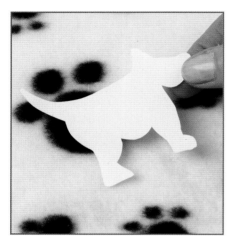

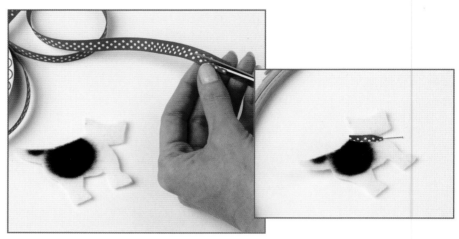

42 Using the template on page 34, create a pattern for the dog. Pin it to some furry fabric, such as this paw print fleece, positioning carefully so that you get a good arrangement of spots. Cut the dog shape using sharp fabric scissors.

43 Create a collar for the dog from spotty ribbon. Depending on the thickness of your ribbon you might want to cut it in half, as shown above left. Cut the collar slightly wider than the width of the dog's neck. Stretch some white organza in an embroidery hoop and pin on the dog and its collar (see above, right).

44 Cut a spade shape from patterned cotton (see page 34 for the template). Pin the spade to a piece of green or yellow organza and cut around it with sharp fabric scissors, making the organza slightly larger all round.

45 Cut out a bucket shape from a piece of cotton using the template on page 34. Cut a piece of pink organza in the same shape but slightly larger, and a piece of wadding in the same shape but smaller. Pin the bucket and spade, under their respective organza pieces, onto the white organza backing – remember to pin the bucket fabric on top of its wadding. Use the template on page 34 to cut out the starfish from orange organza, and pin this on as well.

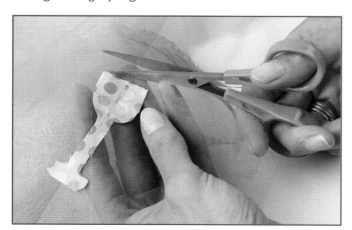

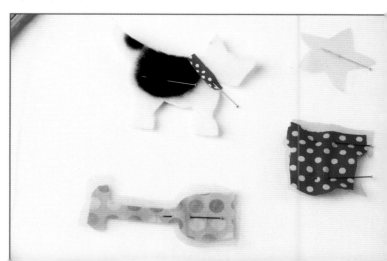

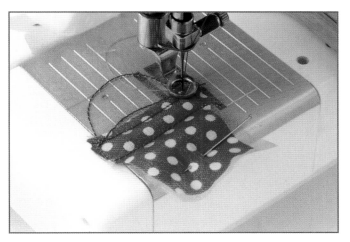

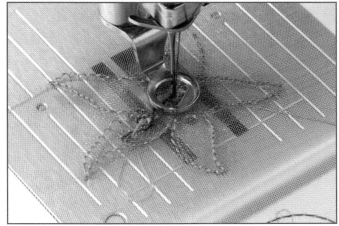

46 To sew the bucket, I used a red top thread and a pink bobbin thread. Stitch a rectangle to create the rim of the bucket then sew a semi-circle of stitches from one side of the rim to the other, around the top of the pink organza – this gives the bucket a three-dimensional feel. Sew a single loop of stitches to form the bucket's handle. Once this is complete, sew down the right-hand side of the bucket, along the bottom and back up to the rim to complete it.

47 Choose an orange top thread and a pink bobbin thread to outline the starfish; sew as close to the edge of the orange organza as you can. To create this lacy effect, loosen the tension on the top thread. Once the outline is complete, change to a dark brown or red top thread and, with the tension on the top thread still loose, fill the centre of the starfish with circular stitches.

48 Use a black machine thread to sew the dog. Start by securing the collar underneath the dog's chin, then work your way clockwise around the inner edge, drawing in the detail of the paws and ears as you go. Once you get back round to your starting point, complete the dog by sewing on the eye and nose. Using turquoise thread, stitch around the spade, a few mm in from the cotton shape's edge.

49 With your stitching complete, take the organza out of the hoop and and cut out your motifs. Cut quite close to the edge of each, but do not worry about being too neat.

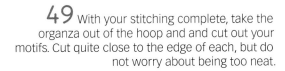

50 Pin all your motifs in place on your picture; to get the arrangement right, try placing them at different heights or partly hiding them in the layers of fabric. Using a sandy coloured, easily disguised thread, hand sew around the outside of the motifs – try to sew on the same line as the machine stitching to make the hand stitches as invisible as possible. Sew right around the edge of the dog and around the parasol pole – space the tiny stitches about 1cm (½in) apart. Sew around the top, curved edge of the parasol. For all the other motifs, sew around the bottom edges only, so that the shapes retain a slightly three-dimensional effect. Don't worry about securing and cutting the thread after you finish each motif: simply take the thread across the back of the fabric as you go.

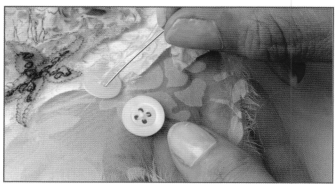

51 To add a final fabric strip to form the foreground, cut a tapering piece of fabric in a sandy colour, measuring about 20cm (8in) wide and between 1cm (½in) and 4cm (1½in) tall, and fray all the edges. Gather the fabric as you did in steps 12 and 13 and pin the ruffled shape in place. With a gold metallic thread in your machine, sew across the bottom of the shape, a few mm from the base, then turn it round and sew back a few mm above this, creating two parallel lines.

52 As a final embellishment, select a few yellow, cream and white buttons and arrange them in the foreground of your picture (see pages 46–47 for inspiration). With a doubled length of cream or white cotton thread, secure each button with a few hand stitches.

53 To create some flying seagulls, restretch the fabric into a hoop with the sky at the centre. Work out where you want your gulls to be and mark the spots with pins. You can create as many as you like, but try to keep them evenly spaced and at different heights; refer to pages 46–47 for guidance. Using a lilac bobbin thread and a dark grey top thread, stitch single-lined curved 'v' shapes where each of your pin markers is, securing the thread by sewing backwards and forwards at the tip of each wing. Once all the gulls are complete, trim away the excess thread. The gulls secure the sky fabric in place. If there are any creases in the organza, lightly iron around the edge, but do not iron the picture itself.

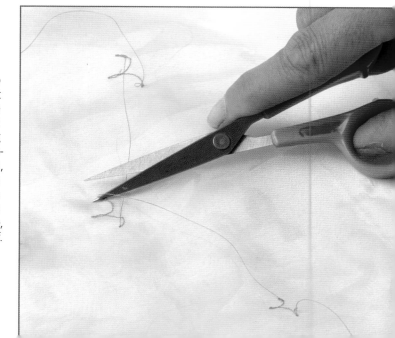

Mounting and framing

Once all of your hard work is over it is time to consider how to mount your embroidery. Having spent time creating layers and texture it is really important to consider how to preserve them through framing. I find that the best way is to do this is to stretch your embroidery on a piece of acid-free mountboard. You simply need to position your picture centrally on the mountboard and sew through it, catching tiny bits of background organza with every stitch. I would recommend using a sturdy needle with a fine point, so that you don't make big holes in the mountboard. Once the embroidery is stretched you can take it to a local framer where it could be window-mounted, or left float-mounted. My other tip at this stage is to choose a deep frame with a slip, which creates a three-dimensional frame for your embroidery to breathe in. If you want your embroidery to have a long lifespan, I would recommend that you don't hang it in direct sunlight, as the fabric might become light-damaged over time.

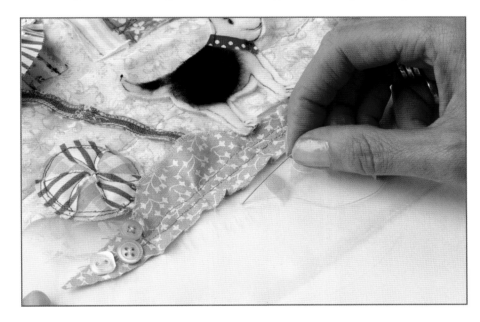

54 Your picture is now complete and ready to be mounted. Choose a piece of white mountboard 5cm (2in) larger all round than your white organza, and a long piece of white or cream cotton thread. Knot the end of your thread and, starting at a corner, secure the piece along all four edges – stretching it taut as you go – using tiny stitches spaced about 5cm (2in) apart. Along the top and two sides, sew around the edge of the organza; along the bottom edge, stitch across the foreground level and try to hide the stitches among the fabric.

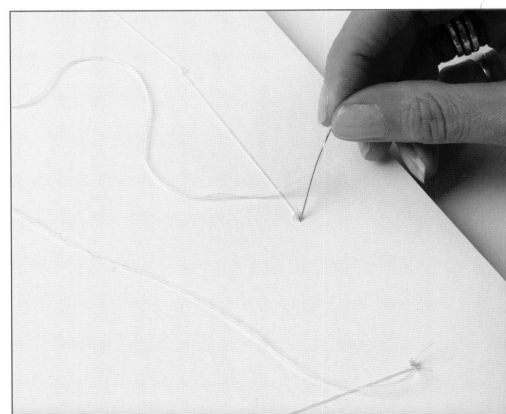

55 Wherever possible, take the stitch back through the same hole to disguise the thread. Once you get back to your starting position, turn the piece over and secure the thread. Your picture is now ready to be framed.

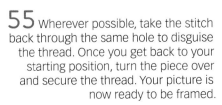

Summer's Day at Southwold
40 x 40cm (16 x 16in)
*I have tried to capture the summertime
scene of candy-striped parasols and
vibrant beach huts against the deep blue
horizon and sandy foreground. The motifs
help to create a whimsical feel.*

Shop fronts

There have been many times that I've had to grab my camera and snap away while wandering through the streets of quaint North Norfolk villages such as Wells-Next-The-Sea and Sheringham. The old-fashioned shop fronts, the stonework and a splash of colour from the late-summer hollyhocks, which stand up so proudly against the cottages, are a real inspiration to me.

One of these shop fronts inspired the delicatessen picture at the old Cley Forge, see right. I really enjoyed making this picture and got carried away in the detail of the baskets of fruits and vegetables on display outside the store. Many of the elements, such as the leeks and mushrooms, were embroidered separately then hand sewn into the baskets at the end. I also used printed fruity fabric, such as the strawberry-print fabric, for a dash of bold colour. If you want to create fruits and vegetables for yourself, but cannot find the right printed fabrics, consider over-dyeing fabrics to get the effect you want (see pages 22–23): the green fabrics used for the leek leaves and cabbages were ones I created myself.

As you will see from the examples on the following pages, shop fronts provide an ideal background on which to apply lots of detail, whether that be pumpkins, onions or even ice cream! If you are planning on creating lots of detail in the motifs, keep the shop front itself relatively simple so that the details can stand out. The colour in these images can be really fun and quirky too, so it is a chance to be bold and creative with your fabric choices.

Cley Forge

55 x 55cm (22 x 22in)

Don't be afraid to use artistic licence: the contrast of the Norfolk flint building with the brightly coloured vegetables, displayed in simple crates and potato sacks, is actually very close to the original scene. However, I have added the windmill in the background to 'locate' the embroidery.

Split Screen Ice Cream

55 x 55cm (22 x 22in)

See page 7.

Allium al Fresco

55 x 55cm (22 x 22in)

This was inspired by a garlic stand at a Royal Horticultural Society show. The whole display was decorated with garlic and planted up with numerous varieties. I made each of the three–dimensional alliums separately, then stitched them onto the background.

Wiveton Hall Farm Shop

55 x 55cm (22 x 22in)

This is such a magical location and a real jewel in the crown of the Norfolk coastline. The drive opens up to a stunning location overlooking marshland with the sea on the horizon where the farm shop is nestled.

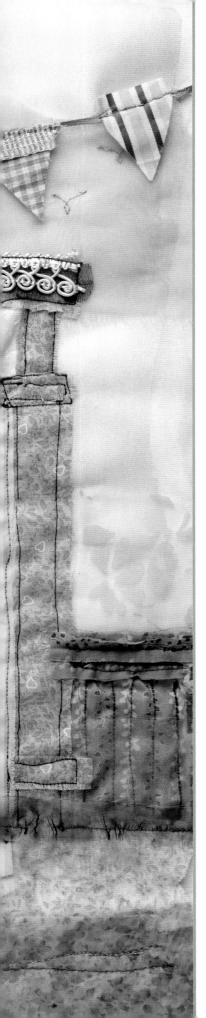

The Chocolate Box at Sheringham

55 x 55cm (22 x 22in)

This old-fashioned sweet shop sits on Sheringham high street, in Norfolk. I enjoyed working the detail of the stonework on the shop front, and embroidering the archway. The bright candy canes and sweet jars are a colourful contrast to the cornflower blue hues of the brickwork. I worked the lace over the top of the embroidery to give depth and a sense of architectural detail.

Cupcake Café

This project draws on many of the techniques that were used on pages 28–45: you will create another dog and ice cream sign, and the shop roofs are made in a similar way to the parasol top, with wadding used to lift their lower edges and make them three-dimensional. This project also introduces some new techniques, such as freehand machine writing. Don't worry if you find the idea of this a bit daunting, as I have some tips to make it easy – see step 16, page 59. Remember to think of the stitching as a key element of the design, and don't be afraid to add in extra embellishments or motifs if you want to. The templates can be found on pages 118–119.

1 Begin by cutting and arranging your background fabrics. On top of your white organza lay down the blue organza central and 5cm (2in) from the top edge; place the cream patterned fabric central and 5cm (2in) from the bottom edge. The brown checked fabric will form the base for your houses and shop front – position it so that its top edge sits slightly higher than half way up. Vertically centre the blue patterned organza on the plain blue organza to form the sky and pin in place. To form the shop window, use template A to create a rectangle of cream fabric. Use template B to cut two strips of brown fabric about 1½ x 10cm (½ x 4in) – as you can see from the example shown below, these lengths can be approximate – you will eventually cover both ends of each strip.

WHAT YOU NEED

hand sewing equipment
sewing machine with darning foot
embroidery hoop
white organza,
    40 x 40cm (16 x 16in)
blue organza,
    30 x 20cm (12 x 8in)
patterned blue organza,
    30 x 8cm (12 x 3in)
cream patterned fabric,
    30 x 10cm (12 x 4in)
brown checked fabric,
    30 x 10cm (12 x 4in)
assorted cotton fabrics
assorted machine threads
metallic gold thread
assorted ribbons
wadding

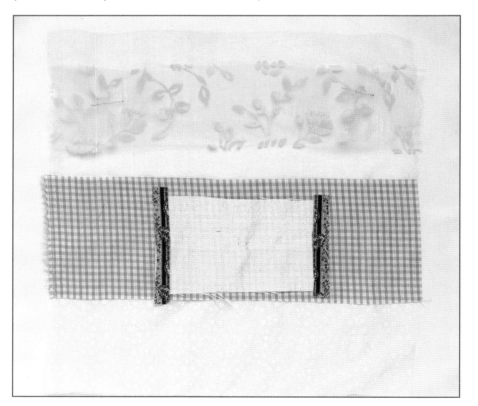

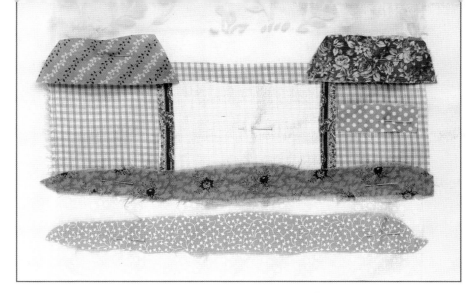

2 Using the templates on pages 118–119, cut two strips of cotton fabric to form the pavement and the foreground (C) – the templates given are 50 per cent of the actual size so you will need to enlarge them. Fray the edges then pin them in position as shown. Next, create two roof shapes (D) and two pieces of wadding – pin the roof shapes in place on top of their pieces of wadding. Finally, use template E to create some decoration for the right-hand house. Pin this in place as shown.

3 Using freehand machine stitching and a dark brown machine thread, sew a single line of stitches across the pavement fabric, about 1cm (½in) from the bottom. Change to a gold metallic thread, and sew a curving, wiggling line backwards and forwards across the foreground piece. Again, sew about 1cm (½in) from the lower edge.

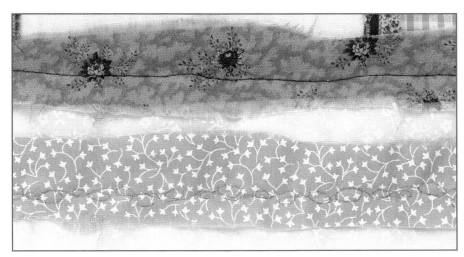

4 From a selection of coloured cottons, use the templates given to create four windows (F and G), two chimneys (H and I), two doorsteps (J), two doors (K) and one porch (L). Pin or glue these in place. The doorsteps should be put in place first – as the doors overlap them slightly – followed by the doors, porch, windows and chimneys. Cut pieces of lace ribbon to fit across the two rooftops and lightly glue them in place.

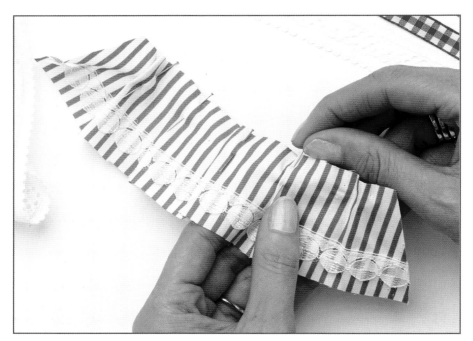

5 Using the template on page 118, cut out a piece of fabric for the central roof (M), and a piece of lace ribbon slightly wider. Pin the ribbon to the roof about 1cm (½in) from the bottom and machine sew it in place using a white machine thread. Trim the ends of the ribbon so that they are flush with the slope of the roof. To make the roof three-dimensional, gather the fabric every 2.5cm (1in) or so, and pin it.

TIP

Sewing the lace before you gather the fabric means that it will sit neatly and won't gape.

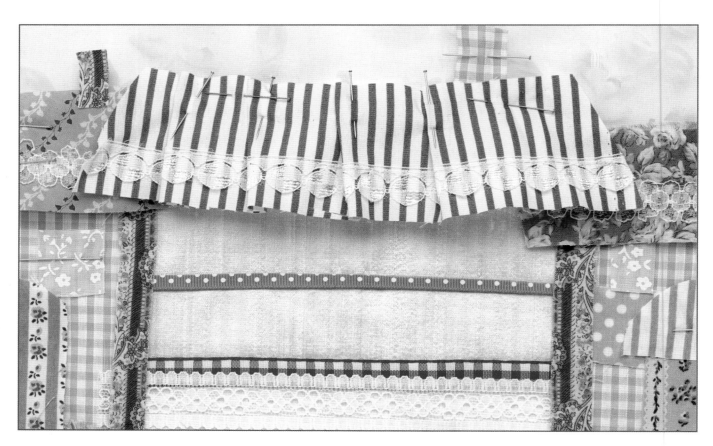

6 Use the template on page 118 to cut a piece of wadding for the central roof. Pin the roof in place on top of its wadding. Cut a 2 x 3cm (¾ x 1¼in) rectangle of fabric to form the chimney and pin this in place as well, tucking the end underneath the roof. Also cut three lengths of ribbon the same width as the shop front and space them as shown above – here I used a grey polka dot, red check and white lace. Secure them with some craft glue and tuck their ends under the upright brown strips of fabric.

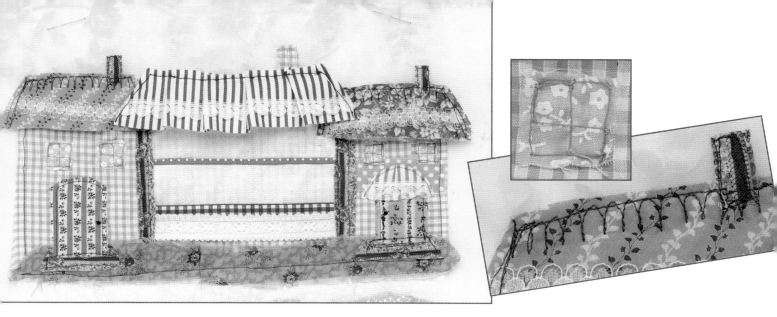

7 With all the pieces in place you might want to add in some extra details: here, a strip of lace ribbon was added to decorate the porch. Using freehand machine stitching and contrasting thread colours, sew all the pieces in place. Sew around the inside edges of the doors and the doorsteps. Sew around the curve of the porch, trapping the lace in place as you go, and sew around the inside of the two vertical brown strips, securing the three ribbons in position. Sew around the inside edge of the windows and then sew a cross on each to create the four window panes.

8 To attach the roofs, sew along the top and two sides of each only. Stitch the two houses first: sew from the bottom left up the side, across the top and down the right side – move the corners of the central roof out of the way as you go. Then sew back the way you came, but instead of a straight line along the top, create a scalloped line, as shown above. For the central roof, simply sew a single line of stiching up the left side, across the top and down the right side, removing the pins carefully as you go. Finally, sew the chimneys in place and sew a vertical line down the outside edge of each house.

9 Using templates O, P, Q, R and S cut out the pieces needed for three cupcakes, one large cake and one strawberry pavlova, with wadding. You will also need to cut a short length of lace ribbon for your cupcakes to sit on. Use the template on page 34, and description on page 40, to create an ice cream sign; you will need a length of lace ribbon to curve around the top edge, and for this project, two short, thin pieces of ribbon to create the legs.

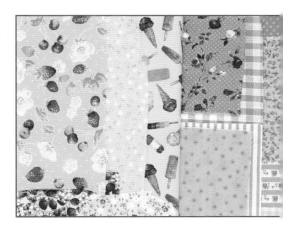

10 Sew a line of contrasting stitching along the centre of the top ribbon, here purple thread was used on the grey polka dot ribbon. Pin your lace and all your cakes into position, remembering to place the wadding underneath the strawberry fabric. Also pin on the ice cream sign – curve the piece of lace around the top of it and position the feet so that they peek out from underneath it.

11 Sew each of the cakes in place using contrasting threads. For the strawberry pavlova, use a red thread and sew several loosely heart-shaped squiggles across the middle of the fabric. For the large cake, sew each element with a different coloured thread: sew two parallel lines of dark pink to form the cakestand; sew the edges of the cake in light pink, sewing a double line of wiggly thread for the jam in the centre, and sew on a tiny circle of red fabric for the cherry.

12 Sew a semi-circle around the top of each cupcake then stitch a tiny circle on top of each to form the cherries. Using purple thread, stitch along the two sides and the bottom of each case, creating a curl or flourish at the top of each side. Finally, use white thread to attach the length of flower lace ribbon that sits beneath the cupcakes. For the ice cream sign (see facing page), sew around the inner edge, starting at the bottom right-hand corner, securing the lace in place as you go. When you get back to your starting position, sew back up the right-hand edge, a few mm in from the first line, to make the sign look three-dimensional. Sew the feet on as shown.

13 Use templates T and U to cut the dog and its ear from fleece fabric, and cut a piece of ribbon for a collar as you did on page 42. Work out where you want the dog to stand then pin it in place. To ensure that you get the elements securely in the correct place, also pin on the collar and ear.

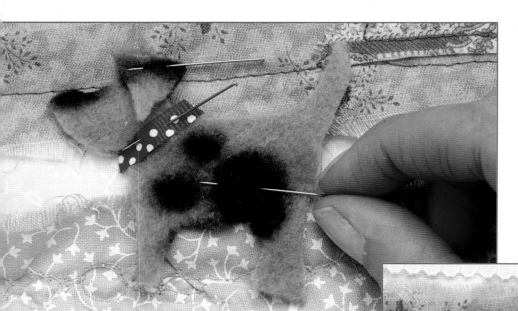

14 Using black machine thread, stitch around the inside edge of the dog, using the same technique as on page 43. Start by securing the top of the dog's collar and then work clockwise, stitching in the scalloped toes and round nose as you go. When you reach the dog's ear, only sew across the top of the triangle, so that the ear lifts up. Finish by stitching on the mouth and eye details.

15 Using template V, cut out the small triangles of fabric that will form your bunting. Mix up colours and patterns – here soft pastel tones have been chosen to complement the rest of the picture. Once you have cut enough to create a line that gently curves across the top of your picture, pin them in place: in this picture, 15 were required. Secure them to the background with a single line of stitching, sewing a few mm down from the wide edge of each triangle.

16 Sew a number of seagulls onto the sky, using the same method as on page 44. Choosing thread colours that will stand out clearly, sew the words 'Ice Cream' onto your ice cream sign and 'Cupcake Café' onto your shop front. Practise on a scrap piece of fabric until you are confident you can get the writing right. Alternatively, if you want a guide, use a dressmaking water-soluble marker to write out the text and then sew over the lines. The pens dry clear and can be removed with water if you make any mistakes. Your piece is now ready to mount following the instructions given on page 45.

Cupcake Café
40 x 40cm (16 x 16in)
This is a great example of how you can use patterned fabric to create realistic imagery and texture, such as the buildings, rooftops and doorways. The candy-striped awning and bright cakes and bunting complement the brickwork, and the dog is the quirky finishing touch!

Teatime treats

I have used teatime imagery for many years and it is still very popular. The theme translates into embroidery really well and a lot of fun can be had creating not only delicious treats, such as French fancies, cream-filled scones or jam tarts, but also vintage-patterned cups, lacy napkins and dainty cakestands. For me, the best part is embellishing cherry-topped cakes, as this gives me a chance to dig out my button collection and finish them off with a little shiny jewel.

The colours can be great fun to work with – for example, mixing vintage rose-print fabrics with bright candy-pink stripes can look really effective. I often appliqué with lace as it is ideal for creating doilies, and it also makes a great trim for tablecloths and napkins, while lamé overlaid with organza can be used really effectively to create shimmering teapots, cakestands and cutlery.

Coffee Morning
30 x 30cm (12 x 12in)

This embroidery differs slightly from my other work as it is built up using cotton and lace, rather than organza, which gives it a slightly bolder feel. I really enjoyed playing around with the different patterned fabrics for the teacups and cakes – the result is almost good enough to eat!

Coffee Time
30 x 30cm (12 x 12in)

These floral fabrics, used with the lacy backgrounds, are some of my favourites for teatime treats. They capture this quintessentially English tradition.

Cupcake
20 x 20cm (8 x 8in)

This is one of my completed embroidery kits – the vibrant mix of colours and patterns works well with the simplicity of the overall design.

Dippy Eggs
30 x 30cm (12 x 12in)
The main idea behind this embroidery was to keep the colourway to 'china blue' and recreate an English breakfast place setting. I combined many different patterned blues to achieve this effect.

Afternoon Tea
56 x 56cm (22 x 22in)

In this piece, I wanted to take the tea party outside. I embroidered the tablecloth with pleated cotton layered with lace. I used lamé sparingly to create the cake plate and spoon, and used a mix of patterned fabrics to create the miniature cakes and a sandwich.

Cakestand and Sugar Bowl

Who could resist this scrummy teatime picture, complete with colourful, button-topped cakes, lacy napkin and sparkling sugar bowl? This picture requires you to create padded and three-dimensional elements, hone the precision of your freehand machine stitching – especially on the base of the cakestand and the teaspoon – and allows you to play around with colours and patterns as you create your cakes. Follow the picture as given, or experiment with the arrangement, colour or number of cakes. The templates are given on pages 120–121.

1 To begin, cut your backing fabrics to the dimensions given in the 'what you need' list. Lay the cream fabric down on top of the white organza, 5cm (2in) from the top and two sides. Next, lay down the polka dot fabric. Its bottom edge should also sit about 5cm (2in) from the bottom of the organza, so it should overlap the cream fabric by about 2cm (¾in). Place the flower lace ribbon about 2.5cm (1in) from the top of the polka dot fabric, and finally place the lace fabric on top of the cream – cut the lace fabric with a scalloped top edge so that some of the cream fabric underneath shows at the top of the picture. Pin all the pieces in position.

WHAT YOU NEED

hand sewing equipment
sewing machine with darning foot
embroidery hoop
white organza,
    40 x 40cm (16 x 16in)
cream background fabric,
    30 x 20cm (12 x 8in)
blue polka dot fabric,
    30 x 12cm (12 x 5in)
flower lace ribbon, 30cm (12in)
lace background,
    30 x 15cm (12 x 6in)
purple-blue organza
silver lamé
assorted machine threads
assorted lace ribbons
gold metallic thread
white crystal organza
5 coloured ribbons
10 patterned cottons
assorted buttons
blue and white striped fabric
wadding

2 Using the templates on pages 120–121, cut out all the shapes needed to make the cakestand, spoon and sugar bowl from silver lamé (A, B, C, D and E) – cut the heart shape so that it is separate from the central pole. Pin A, C, D and E onto blue-purple organza and cut around them, making the organza shapes a few mm larger all round. To create an organza accent for shape B, cut template G from blue-purple organza. Cut a small piece of wadding (template F) to fit underneath the sugar bowl.

3 Arrange the pieces as shown – with the organza shapes on top of the silver lamé and the wadding in place underneath the sugar bowl shape – and pin them in place, leaving the base of the cakestand unpinned. Make sure that you are happy with the spacing between the lace ribbon and the sugar bowl – if not, move either accordingly. Lift up the bottom of the cakestand, fold it back on itself and pin it out of the way. Using a mid-blue machine thread, sew a straight line across the polka dot fabric, about 1cm (½in) from the top. Change to a white thread and machine along the flower lace ribbon to hold it in place. Fold the bottom of the cakestand back down and pin.

4 Cut two lengths of flower lace ribbon slightly longer than each of the plates on the stand. Pin them in place, curving them around the bottom of each plate. Also cut a length of lace ribbon slightly wider than the sugar bowl and pin this to its top edge (see step 5 for reference).

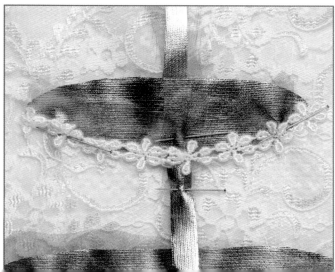

5 Using a dark blue machine thread, stitch around each shape to outline and give definition. See right and below for reference. Create small scalloped stitches around the outer edge of the heart and the plates to create a lacy outline; trap the lace ribbons in place as you go. With gold metallic thread, sew some five-petalled flower shapes on to the background lace. Dot them about at random.

6 The sugar that sits in the bowl is a ruched piece of white crystal organza tucked behind the silver lamé. Cut template H from the white crystal organza and fold it in half lengthways. Using white cotton thread, sew a loose running stitch along the length of its bottom edge, creating a tube shape, and then pull it tight to gather the fabric into ruffles. Tuck it in place and hand sew in position.

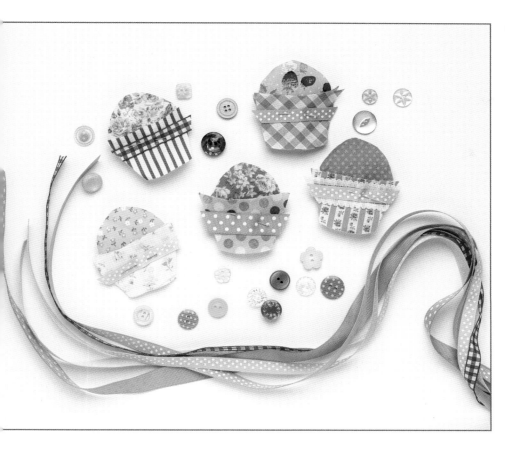

7 Using templates I and J you will need to create five cupcakes. Choose a selection of contrasting fabrics and ribbons, and play around until you are happy with your colour and pattern combinations. Cut a piece of wadding for each cupcake that is the same shape but slightly smaller than the overall size, using template K. Pin your cakes, cases, wadding and ribbons together.

TIP

As the cupcakes are only small, this is the ideal time to use up any scraps of material you have lying around.

8 Pin your cupcake shapes and their wadding in place on the stand.

9 Sew around the top of each cupcake – a few mm from the edge – using brown or orange thread. Choose a contrasting thread colour for each cupcake case. Create a curl at the top of the right side then machine down the right side, across the bottom and up the left-hand side, creating a mirror image of your first curl at the top. Sew back the way you came – close to your line of stitches – and as you cross the bottom of the case, sew a deeply scalloped line instead of a straight one. Select five interesting, contrasting buttons and hand sew these onto your cupcakes using doubled lengths of colourful cotton thread.

10 From stripy blue fabric, cut a parallelogram shape using template L. Also cut out the wadding shape given. Cut two lengths of lace ribbon long enough to cover the bottom and right-hand edges; pin the lace to the front of the bottom edge and to the back of the right-hand edge.

TIP

In this example, the right side of the fabric will be folded in on itself. If you want the right side of your fabric to show on the outside, simply turn your fabric over before you pin on your lace ribbon.

11 Using a soft pink machine thread, sew around the four sides of your handkerchief, a few mm from the edge, trapping the lace ribbon in place. Fold the handkerchief over, sandwiching the wadding in the middle, then hand sew it in position on your picture; choose a pale thread colour and use tiny stitches around the bottom and right-hand side. Your picture is now ready to mount: follow the instructions on page 45.

Cakestand and Sugar Bowl
40 x 40cm (16 x 16in)

*Have fun using areas of lamé and
mixing up patterned fabrics with quirky
buttons and brightly coloured ribbons!*

Country garden

Working with garden imagery is a great opportunity to put all of your embroidery skills and techniques into practice: from building up soft layers of colour and texture for a shrubbery, to incorporating printed floral fabrics for flowerbeds or climbing plants. The best thing about garden pictures is the scope for detail – try to mirror some of the beauty and intricacy of the plants, flowers and vegetables through your choices of fabric, your techniques and the way you use your stitching. The cabbages shown right, for example, make gorgeous subjects for embroidery, with their extravagant, abundant leaves and padded, embroidered hearts, while the flowerbeds in the image on pages 80–81 are a riot of colour, as a number of floral fabrics vie for attention.

As well as being aesthetically pleasing, gardens make the perfect subject for a really personal image or gift. I have taken endless photographs of friends' gardens, from Norfolk in England to Paxos in Greece, as it is so easy to transform a much-loved garden into a work of art!

Potting Shed

56 x 56cm (22 x 22in)

This elegant potting shed is surrounded by a rainbow of colourful flowers and vegetables. This scene is the ideal opportunity to create a mix of textures, from the padded cabbages and raised purple flowers to the delicate rambling roses.

Rosa's Washing Line
56 x 56cm (22 x 22in)

The washing line is very whimsical and is lovely to embroider as you can contrast the precise, neat shapes of the washing blowing in the breeze against the relaxed and informal garden backdrop.

Olive Grove in Paxos
56 x 56cm (22 x 22in)

I changed my colour palette from English country garden to the olive tones of the Mediterranean: the bright pink of the hammock provides a lovely contrast to the blue-green tones elsewhere.

Secret Doorway
56 x 56cm (22 x 22in)

There are a number of different textures created in this piece, from the ruffled thatched roof to the large, part-embroidered leaves. I used one of my favourite laced green ribbons to represent the ferns and cut out floral fabric to create a climbing rose around the door of the cottage.

Country Cottage
56 x 56cm (22 x 22in)

See page 19.

Cottage Garden

This country scene draws on many of the techniques used in previous projects: wadding is used to create a three-dimensional roof, the foreground pieces are frayed and gathered to add depth and texture, and organza pieces are layered with cotton to add shadow and depth of colour. The key feature of this piece is the stitching – here swirling curls of stitching are used to create the tree's foliage; the climbing rose around the cottage door is picked out in flower- and leaf-like stitches, and the carrot tops and leafy foliage are sewn with organic, flowing lines. The templates for this project are given on pages 122–123.

1 Start by cutting and arranging your background fabrics: lay the white organza down first then place the blue and green plain organzas on top, overlapping the green over the blue by about 5cm (2in) to give a 5cm (2in) border of white organza all round. Fray the edges of the blue and green patterned strips then position them as shown. Pin all the pieces in place.

WHAT YOU NEED

hand sewing equipment
sewing machine with darning foot
embroidery hoop
white organza, 40 x 40cm (16 x 16in)
blue organza, 30 x 22cm (12 x 9in)
patterned blue organza,
   30 x 10cm (12 x 4in)
green organza, 30 x 15cm (12 x 6in)
patterned green organza,
   30 x 10cm (12 x 4in)
assorted fabrics
flower fabric or ribbon
gold metallic thread
assorted machine threads
wadding
lace ribbon
fern-like ribbon or trim

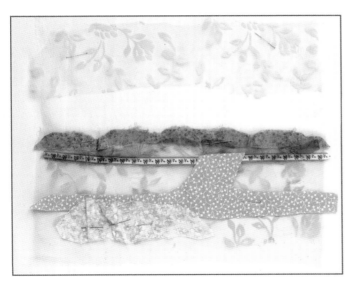

2 Pin flower ribbon, or a strip of flowered fabric cut to 30 x 1cm (12 x ½in), about 2cm (¾in) from the top edge of the patterned green organza. Use template A, given at 50 per cent, to cut a piece of green cotton and a piece of green organza; fray them both. Layer them as shown, ensuring that the green organza overlaps both the bottom of the green cotton and the top of the fabric or ribbon strip. Gather and ruffle the cotton and organza slightly as you pin them in place (see page 32). Using the templates on pages 122–123, cut the path and the foreground shapes (B and C) from brown and cream patterned fabrics and pin them in place as shown: the top of the path should overlap the fabric or ribbon strip, and the foreground should overlap the path. Ruffle the cream foreground as you pin it.

3 Prepare your machine for freehand machine stitching and with a green machine thread, sew a zigzag, grass-like pattern on top of the green organza – ensure that the zigzags are deep enough to secure both the green cotton and the fabric or ribbon strip in place at the same time. Once this is secure, use a gold metallic thread to attach the path. Starting on the left-hand side, sew a winding, wiggling line of stitches, a few mm from the top edge, up to the point where the path meets the horizon. From here, sew a single line of straight stitches around the shape until you reach the right-hand side. You do not need to sew the lower edge. With brown threads and wiggly, curving stitches, sew the foreground in place, about 1cm (½in) from the bottom.

4 Using templates E, F and G cut out the pieces for the cottage's roof, windows and door from patterned cottons; cut a piece of cream fabric about 12 x 12cm (5 x 5in) square to create the cottage wall. Also use template E to cut a piece of wadding to fit under the roof.

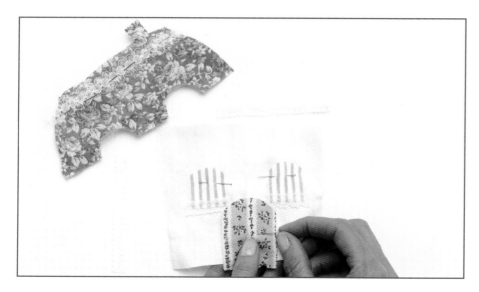

5 Cut a piece of lace ribbon long enough to cover the length of the roof. Pin the lace, the roof fabric and the wadding together. Pin the windows and door in place on the cottage. Cut pieces of lace ribbon to fit down each side of the cottage and under each window – stick them in place using a glue stick. Pin the whole cottage in position on the background – the front door should line up with the path. Cut a rectangle about 5 x 1cm (2 x ½in) to form the doorstep and pin it in place in front of the cottage.

6 Use templates H, I and J to cut out the pieces of the tree: cut the trunk (J) from brown patterned cotton, the canopy (H) from green patterned cotton, and then a piece of organza (I) that will provide some shadow. Pin these in place on the background (see pages 88–89 for guidance), hiding the base of the trunk behind the foreground fabric. The green organza should sit on the left-hand side of the canopy, and should slightly overhang the edge of the tree.

7 Using a light brown thread, stitch up either side of the cottage and sew a rectangle for each windowsill – securing all the lace ribbon in place. Create the windows as you did on page 57: sew around the inside edge of each window first, then sew two bisecting lines across the centre of each to make the window panes. With a dark brown thread, sew a rectangle around the inside edge of the doorstep. For the roof, start at the bottom left corner and sew up, across the top and down the right-hand side. Return to the top and sew a scalloped line of stitches that is deep enough to hold the lace in place. Sew the chimney as shown to give it a three-dimensional look. With blue thread, sew around the sides and top of the door, then stitch six vertical stripes on it. Finally, pin 2cm (¾in) high frayed pieces of green organza to the wall on either side of the front door.

8 Using brown machine thread, sew up the left-hand side of the trunk and then sew a single line of stitches up each branch; complete the trunk by sewing down the right-hand side back to the base. Place a green thread in your machine and sew curly spirals of stitching to secure the green cotton and organza and to give the impression of fluffy foliage.

9 Use template K to create four foliage shapes and template L to make one flowerbed shape – try to find fabrics with leaves and flowers on them. Fray the edges of the flowerbed fabric. Cut four lengths of green, fern-like trim between 6–10cm (2½–4in) long.

10 You will need to make three carrots. Each carrot requires two pieces of patterned cotton (templates M and N) and an organza top layer (also template M); the leaves require a cotton base and an organza top layer, both created using template O. Using a glue stick, secure the two carrot cottons together then lay the organza piece on top. To make the leaves, gather and ruffle the cotton backing and the organza top layer and pin them together.

11 Choose a rose-print fabric and cut a climbing rose shape that will fit over the door and up the side of the cottage; if your fabric has a green background, try to cut some green leaf-like shapes surrounding the flowers. Use the detail on the fabric to inform your shape – try to make it look as natural as possible. Pin in place, allowing it to slightly overlap the edge of the door.

12 Work out where you would like your carrots to sit, then pin them in place. To create the illusion that they are growing from the ground, position them so that you can tuck their ends behind either the foreground fabric or the path fabric when you come to sew.

13 Arrange your four foliage shapes closely together on top of the path – their top edges should overlap the cottage slightly. Pin them in place. The fern-like ribbon should curl at the ends to resemble real ferns. When you are happy with their general position, pin their stalks in place and then pin the curled ends.

14 Sew the plants and ferns using two or three different green threads. For the plants, sew up their central stems, creating a gentle wiggle in your stitches to make the plants look as though they are moving in the wind; 'draw' in a few leaves here and there. To give the ferns a three-dimensional look, only sew them at the top and bottom (with the exception of the smallest fern). Sew them slowly and carefully so that you can achieve as curly a shape as possible. Ruffle the flowerbed shape and pin it so that it overlaps the bottom of the foliage. Using green thread, secure the fabric with a grass-like zigzag about 1cm (½in) from the bottom.

15 To attach the climbing roses to the cottage, pick out the details in the fabric. Use a matching pink thread to sew rose-like shapes in the centre of some of the flowerheads. Use a bright green thread to pick out some of the leaf detail. There is no need to sew every rose and leaf – just sew until you are happy that the rose fabric is attached evenly and securely.

16 Machine stitch the carrots in place by sewing over the shadow shape. Sew the carrot tops with bright green thread – follow the direction of the leaves and then end each line of stitching with a curl. Don't worry about stitching over all the leaves, you still want them to be fairly three-dimensional. Finish the piece by sewing on some flying birds, as on page 45. Your piece is now ready to mount: follow the instructions on page 45.

Cottage Garden

40 x 40cm (16 x 16in)

This piece makes a real feature of its printed fabrics: using leaf-pattern fabric for the tree, rose-print fabric for the climbing roses and flower-print fabrics for the flowerbeds creates a lovely effect.

Animals

I grew up surrounded by animals, and having children has been a great excuse to build up my own menagerie. Animals provide a wonderful source of inspiration, and capturing the likeness of a pet in an artwork can be really very special. But as simple as they often look, animals can be quite tricky subjects to embroider – if you oversimplify them they can look too cartoon-like, while details like eyes can be hard to get right and can even look a little scary if you try to make them look realistic. It can be hard to make minimal look easy, so you will probably need to practise, practise, practise!

There are many effective types of fabrics available that can be used to create animals, such as fur fabric and patterned fleeces – I layer them up and add dark organzas for shading over the top – or lace fabric for textures such as chicken feathers and sheep's wool, see page 92. Use dark cotton to embroider eyes and other facial features. If the features don't go according to plan then I would recommend adding a new piece of fabric over the top and trying again!

Hare
40 x 40cm (16 x 16in)

To create the hare I made the head and body separately. Lace was used sparingly on the body, and combined with softer pink fabrics to create the large, delicate ears. The hare's whiskers are lengths of thread couched down in the middle so that they hang loosely. The cute, multi-coloured toadstools are nestled into the grassy foreground. The over-dyed, printed cotton grass is subtle and blends well with the rest of the embroidery.

Sheep
40 x 40cm (16 x 16in)

The detail of the sheep's faces was embroidered over the white satin and lace used to create their woolly coats. The sheep are fairly simple, so I created other detail within the piece – the fence, robin and tree – to build up the scene.

Owl
40 x 40cm (16 x 16in)

The owl is made from a real mixture of colourful fabrics and lace, and I used two flower shapes cut from lace ribbon to create its eyes. The fabric used for the tree is really effective: I used a stripey, patterned fabric to create the look of the trunk's texture, and assorted green printed cottons to create the leaves.

Hedgehog
40 x 40cm (16 x 16in)

This hedgehog is nestled into a grassy foreground made of ruffled and frayed hand–dyed cottons. The toadstools are padded out for a three–dimensional effect and there are layers of lace embroidered over the hedgehog to form his spiky texture. The pink butterflies add a whimsical, delicate touch.

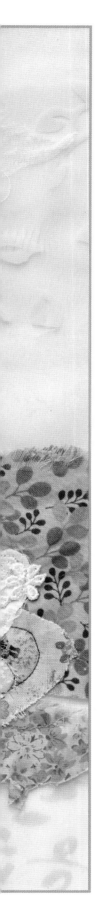

Geese
40 x 40cm (16 x 16in)

The white geese in this embroidery really stand out against the rich dark green background. They were worked up on layers of white satin with white stitching. The green and red fruit-print fabric was perfect for creating the tree, and I picked out the details with my embroidery.

Suffolk Pig in Pumpkin Patch
30 x 30cm (12 x 12in)

This little pig was one that I spotted at Wiveton Hall in autumn, snuffling through the pumpkins. I layered up pink satin, velvet and organza to create his body, then defined it with pink stitching.

Hen House

Use your stitching to bring each of the chickens to life – they are the focus of this piece, from their fluffy, lacy bottoms to their scalloped, ruffled wings. Practise sewing a few beforehand if you need to, to make sure you are happy with the effects you can create. When you come to sew the birds, bear in mind that the feet, beaks, combs and wattles are very small and fiddly, so you might want to sew on these smaller details by hand. The hen house itself comprises a lot of different pieces, so make life easy for yourself by using a glue stick to secure the pieces together before you sew; they can be pulled apart and re-glued if you aren't happy with your arrangement. The templates for this project are given on pages 124–125.

1 Start by cutting and arranging your background fabrics: lay the white organza down first then place the blue and green plain organza on top, overlapping the green over the blue by about 5cm (2in) to give a 5cm (2in) border of white organza all round. Fray the edges of the blue and green patterned strips then position them as shown. Pin all the pieces in place.

WHAT YOU NEED

hand sewing equipment
sewing machine with darning foot
embroidery hoop
white organza, 40 x 40cm (16 x 16in)
blue organza, 30 x 22cm (12 x 9in)
green organza, 30 x 15cm (12 x 6in)
blue patterned organza,
    30 x 10cm (12 x 4in)
green patterned organza,
    30 x 12cm (12 x 5in)
assorted fabrics
assorted threads
lace ribbon

2 Use the templates on pages 124–125 to create shapes A, B, C and D (A and B are given at 50 per cent of actual size). Create shape A and two shape Cs from patterned cotton; cut shape B and two shape Ds from green organza. Also cut a 32 x 1.5cm (12½ x ½in) strip of floral fabric. Arrange the pieces as shown above: lay shape A down first and then pin the tree highlights and organza on top. Place shape B so that most of it overlaps shape A, then place the fabric strip below this.

3 Using freehand machine stitching and a green thread, sew a grass-like zigzag of stitches along the strip of green organza. Ensure that the stitches go high and low enough to catch both the floral fabric strip and shape A as you go. To create a sense of life and movement within the tree, sew large curling spirals all over for its foliage, including on top of the organza. Make a feature of the curls by sewing a few with a darker green thread. Secure the trunk with a parallel line of green stitches.

4 Cut out the pieces for the hen house using templates E (x1), F (x2), G (x1), H (x1), I (x1), J (x3) and K (x3). To create the side of the hen house cut a piece of fabric 6 x 9cm (2½ x 3½in); to create the window, cut a piece of fabric 4 x 5cm (1½ x 2in), and cut two 5cm (2in) lengths of ribbon that will sit on top of it. Try to use neutral coloured, striped or checked fabrics, if you can, as this gives the impression of slats of wood. Use craft glue to stick them together as shown.

5 Pin the hen house onto the background as shown. Pin the three steps in front. Use templates L and M to create the two foreground shapes. Fray the edges of each, gather the fabric and pin on the ruffled shapes.

6 Sew a line of light brown stitching up the left-hand side of the hen house, then change to dark brown thread and sew vertical lines up the right-hand edge and the rear edge. Sew the roof in place: sew along the rooftop and around the inside edge of each beam; create a triangle detail at the front where the beams meet. Sew around the inside edge of all the other shapes, creating four panes of glass in the window.

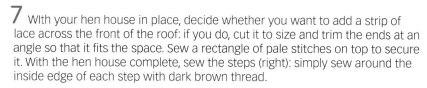

7 With your hen house in place, decide whether you want to add a strip of lace across the front of the roof: if you do, cut it to size and trim the ends at an angle so that it fits the space. Sew a rectangle of pale stitches on top to secure it. With the hen house complete, sew the steps (right): simply sew around the inside edge of each step with dark brown thread.

8 Using the templates on pages 124–125 cut one set of N, O and P, two sets of Q and R, and six legs (S) from neutral coloured cottons. Also cut out combs and wattles for the two standing chickens and a comb from red cotton for the sitting chicken (see template T). Cut two pieces of shape U from organza. Cut a small amount of lace ribbon and stick it to the back of shapes O and P using a glue stick. Cut tiny triangles of grey fabric to form two beaks (see template T). With so many small pieces of fabric, you may find it easiest to lay out each chicken's pieces together.

9 The bodies of the chickens are composed of three layers: the standing chickens have a cotton body layer, an organza layer on top, and then the wing; the sitting chicken has a cotton tail, which peeks out from underneath the cotton body, with the wing on top. Pin all these layers together. Use a glue stick to attach the combs, wattles and beaks to the chickens' heads. Glue the legs to the back of the chickens so that they poke out from underneath. Before you attach the legs of the sitting chicken, cut them slightly shorter, so that only the feet poke out from under the body, see page 100 for reference.

10 Work out exactly where you want your chickens to be and pin them in place.

11 Cut out a circle of patterned cotton approximately 2.5cm (1in) in diameter to form the sun, and a piece of organza that is slightly larger all round. Pin these in place on your background, then sew around the inside of the cotton circle twice, using a complementary thread colour, and making one loop slightly smaller than the other.

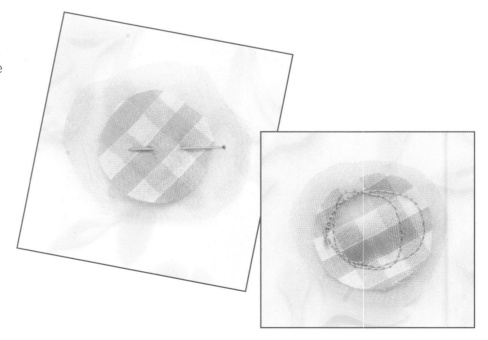

12 Using a green machine thread, freehand machine stitch the foreground pieces. Sew a wiggling, grass-like zigzag of stitches across the middle of each.

13 Take great care when sewing your chickens. Using complementary thread colours, sew around the edge of each chicken, 'drawing' in the feather shapes on the tail and wings. Sew the beaks in dark brown, the legs and feet in dark grey, and the combs and wattles in red. Hand sew the eyes using black thread. If you feel that the wings look too flat, add another ruffled wing shape on top, as shown below. Finally, machine sew a few flying birds in the sky to complete your piece ready for mounting (see page 45).

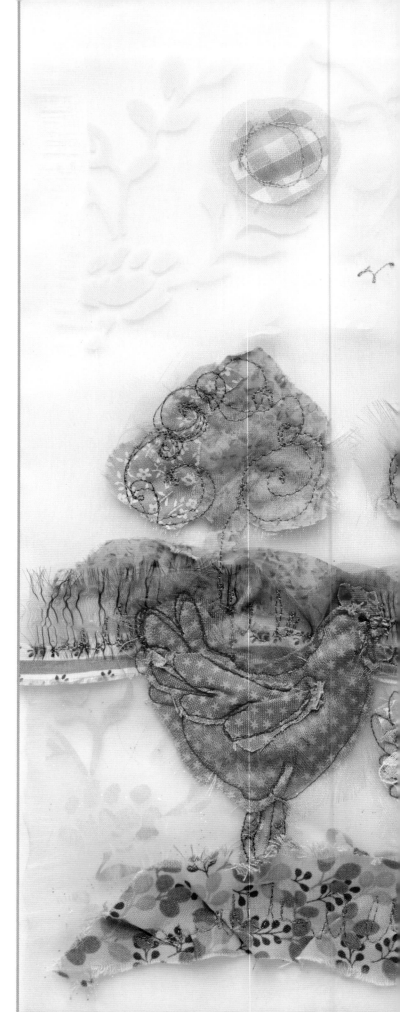

Hen House
40 x 40cm (16 x 16in)

*The layers of fabric on the chickens'
bodies should be ruffled up to replicate
soft, fluffy feathers. If the features of the
chickens don't work out when you first
embroider them, try adding a new piece
of fabric over the top and simply try again.*

Seaside

I have spent many years living in Norfolk and Suffolk, and still take long family walks along the beautiful and hugely inspiring coastline. The most important advice I can give you when designing your own seaside scene is to keep your eyes peeled for detail: allow the little things to catch your eye. It could be light shimmering on the water, the contrast of turquoise rope against orange buoys, pebbles on the beach and sand dunes, or even a seal bobbing up in the harbour. The important thing is to try and integrate these kinds of details into your pictures, as they are what will bring them to life.

Coastal scenes are ideal for my style of work, as the sky, beach and water suit lots of subtle layers of colour and texture, which can be contrasted with detailed areas such as buckets and spades or chalk boards outside fish shops and fishing shacks. Try to bring a few areas of bright or bold colour into each piece to contrast with the soft blue tones of the sea and sky – beach huts provide a great opportunity to add fun, bright colours and patterns. Try to think creatively about the way you introduce embellishments, too – why not create shells on the beach with buttons or tiny pearls, or make shimmering fish, shells or starfish from lamé or metallic thread?

Southwold Pier (above)
41 x 86cm (16 x 34in)

Beach Huts (right)
41 x 86cm (16 x 34in)

These long embroideries are ideal for replicating the big Suffolk skies and blue horizons. I especially like the foreground motifs, which add some summer fun to each scene.

105

Fishing Boat at Aldeburgh
56 x 56cm (22 x 22in)

This embroidery incorporates so many details that I love: the three-dimensional boat and lobster pots, the cornflower blue foreground contrasted with the orange crabs, and the embroidered lettering.

Southwold Green
56 x 56cm (22 x 22in)

Here I have taken some artistic license: I've incorporated the lighthouse and seaside of Southwold, Suffolk, and brought in elements of the village green and cottages, using patterned fabric to recreate the brickwork and grass.

Samantha K's
56 x 56cm (22 x 22in)

*I normally try to avoid using black in my embroideries,
but in this scene I was inspired by the fish shacks down at
Southwold harbour, Suffolk, which are painted in traditional
black. I also worked words into the embroidery, to create
the feel of the produce for sale at the shop.*

DOROTHY
MAY
IP SW
THY
Sea
Lobster
Kipper

The Fish Shack at Aldeburgh
41 x 86cm (16 x 34in)

This is my favourite sea-themed embroidery so far, not only because the location is so special to me, but because it combines all of my favourite embroidery techniques. I especially like the cornflower blue horizon, broken up with the stark outline of the fishing boats and fish shack on the shingle beach. The boats are embroidered as separate three-dimensional elements then sewn onto the background. I have used over-dyed patterned cotton, frayed and ruffled, to create the sand dunes and grasses, and embroidered 'fishy' words to add atmosphere.

Harbour Scene

The key feature of this seaside scene is the illusion of depth: it contains a large number of cotton and organza layers, amongst which a velvet seal is half hidden. The careful colour graduation helps to give the illusion of distance, the foreshortened jetty leads the eye into the centre of the picture, and the three-dimensional boat leaps out towards the viewer. The templates for this project can be found on pages 126–127.

1 Begin by cutting and arranging your background fabrics. On top of your white organza, lay your blue organza so that it creates a white 5cm (2in) border along the top and two sides, then lay your patterned blue organza slightly higher than half way up it. Place the patterned cream cotton below, creating a 5cm (2in) white border along the bottom and two sides. Create the sand by cutting a piece of fabric 30cm (12in) wide that tapers from 10cm (4in) tall at one end to 15cm (6in) tall at the other. Align the top edge of this with the top edge of the cream fabric. Pin.

WHAT YOU NEED

hand sewing equipment
sewing machine with
    darning foot
embroidery hoop
white organza,
    40 x 40cm (16 x 16in)
plain blue organza,
    30 x 20cm (12 x 6in)
patterned blue organza,
    30 x 6cm (12 x 2½in)
cream patterned fabric,
    30 x 10cm (12 x 6in)
assorted fabrics
assorted threads
gold metallic thread
wadding
lace ribbon

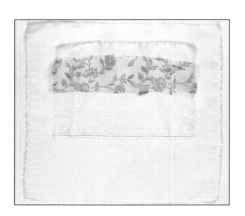

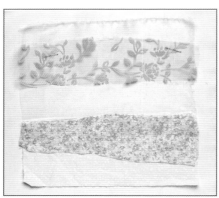

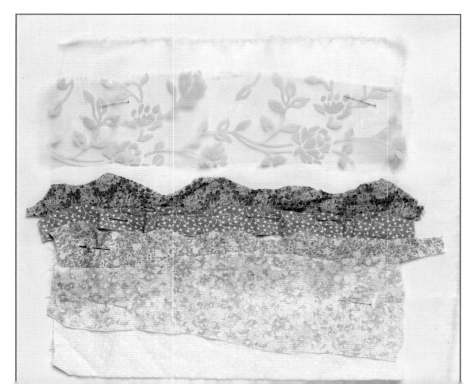

2 To create the sea, cut a piece of blue patterned fabric about 30cm (12in) wide that tapers from 7cm (3in) tall on the left side to 3cm (1¼in) tall on the right side. Slip it under the yellow sand fabric so that about half of it is covered. Using template A, cut the sandbank shape from brown cotton, and using template B cut the island from green cotton. Gather the fabric and pin these ruffled shapes above the blue of the sea, overlapping their top and bottom edges slightly.

3 Cut out the island's organza shape in green and pin it so that it overlaps both the green island and the brown sandbank. Use template C to create a floral foreground shape and a white patterned organza shape. Gather the floral shape and pin it in the bottom left-hand corner. Gather the white shape and pin it directly above the floral shape so that it slightly overlaps the sea. Cut a strip of dark blue cotton, 30 x 1cm (12 x ½in) and position this between the sandbank and the sea – you may need to unpin and move your fabrics slightly to achieve this. Finally, cut another piece of blue patterned organza to roughly cover the whole of the sea area. Pin these in place.

4 Using gold metallic thread, sew a grass-like zigzag across the bottom of the floral foreground shape, about 1cm (½in) from the bottom. Sew the bottom edge of the patterned white organza shape in place with a few thick bands of blue stitching (shown below).

5 Sew the layers in place using stitches and colours that reflect the subject matter: use a green, grass-like zigzag across the organza island. With a gold metallic thread, sew a curving, wiggling line across the centre of the brown sandbank. Also sew a gold wiggling line across the foreground to suggest a pebbly beach – start about 2.5cm (1in) from the right-hand side and sew about a third of the way across. To sew the water, sew long, undulating lines of thread across the darker layers, and short, thick bands of stitching closer to the shore.

6 Use the templates provided to create the pieces for the jetty (D–H), sailing boat (I, J, K and N) and seal (O and P). Also cut wadding for the boat and sails (indicated on template), and two boat shadows (templates L and M) – one from cotton and one from blue organza. Use grey velvet to create the seal's head and tail, and then use the same templates to cut two corresponding pieces of white organza.

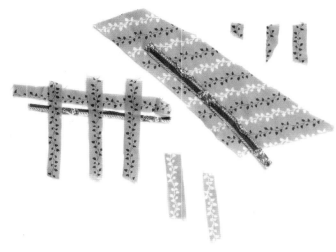

7 Tuck the seal's head and tail under the ruffled piece of patterned white organza so that a few mm are hidden. Arrange the seal's organza shapes on top of their corresponding velvet shapes and pin them in place. Attach the jetty: get the main jetty piece in position first then arrange the supporting beams around it. Tuck the shortest supports (H) under the fabric and overlap all the others. Two of the horizontal beams (E) sit behind the tallest vertical supports (F).

8 Layer and pin the boat's cotton and organza shadows in place first then pin the boat and its wadding on top so that they slightly overlap. Cut a strip of ribbon about 9cm (3½in) long to form the mast and tuck the end of this behind the boat. Pin on the sails, on top of their wadding, securing a piece of lace ribbon on top of each. Finally, attach the flag at the top of the mast.

9 Using brown top and bobbin threads, outline the elements of the jetty. Sew the three shortest supports (H) first, then sew around the sides and top of the jetty shape, trapping the brown strip in place as you sew the left-hand side. Sew the two medium supports (G) next, creating a circle on the top of each to make them look three-dimensional. Ensure that you sew the horizontal supports (E) before sewing the three tallest supports (F). Carefully fold them out of the way while you sew. To finish, sew an extra wiggle of gold stitches in the top right of the sand fabric, to hold it in place.

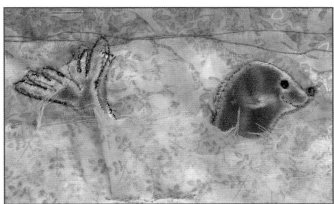

10 Using a light grey top thread with a lilac bobbin, outline the seal's head. Sew the nose as you do the outline, then go back and sew the mouth and eye. Outline the seal's tail – sewing in the scalloped line as shown – with the same grey thread as used for the head, then change to a slightly darker grey thread and re-sew the scalloped parts of the tail, and the eye and nose, for extra emphasis.

11 With dark blue thread, sew right around the inside of the boat, a few mm from the edge. For detail, sew two extra lines that run the length of the boat – one red, one blue – and to make the boat look slightly three-dimensional, sew another line up the right-hand side of the boat, as close to the edge as you can. Sew the mast, sails and flag with gold metallic thread – use a brown bobbin thread for the mast; white bobbin thread for the sails. From the bottom of the mast, sew up to the top of the flag and back down. Sew down the right-hand side of each sail, along the bottom, and then up the left-hand side as far as the lace; for the left-hand sail, continue the line across the sail.

12 To secure the boat's shadow, use silver metallic thread to sew a ripple-like stitch in the wake of the boat. Use brown thread to sew the number '54' onto the right-hand sail.

13 To make the second boat, stretch a piece of white organza in an embroidery hoop. Use template R to cut a piece of white silk for the beached boat's end. Pin this to the white organza with a piece of lace and a strip of striped fabric across its width. Using blue thread, sew around the inside edge of the shape. Remove the organza from the hoop and cut out the shape.

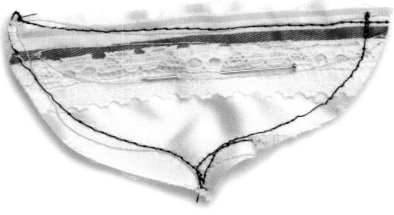

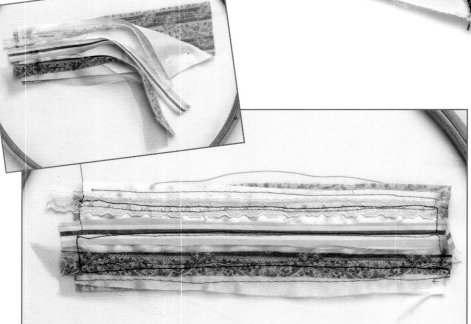

14 Using template S, cut two pieces of fabric: one brown and one white. Lay the brown piece face down, then place the white on top, face up. Using the template as a guide, cut two strips of patterned cotton, one length of lace ribbon and one strip of organza. Arrange these on top of the white fabric, overlapping all the edges slightly, and secure them by sewing around the inside edge and sewing a few stripes along the length.

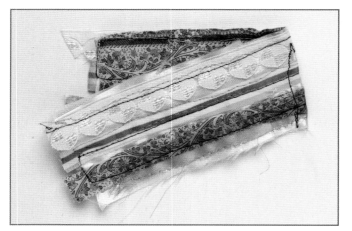

15 Lay the fabric strip with the brown side facing up, then fold the right-hand edge over and down, as shown above. Machine a line of stitches up the right-hand edge to hold the shape in place. Flip the fabric over, so that the shorter side is on top, and twist the top flap up so that it balloons slightly, then hand sew a line of stitches to hold it in place.

16 Pin the end of the boat onto the end of the short flap. Make sure that the two top edges align, and overlap the two pieces by about 2cm (¾in). Cut a thin piece of wadding, about 8 x 2cm (3 x ¾in) big, and slot it between the two layers of the boat.

17 If you want to create a number or name for your beached boat, stretch a piece of white organza in a hoop and freehand machine stitch the letters or numbers you want. Remove the organza from the hoop and cut out the numbers. Using white thread, stitch the number to the boat; stitch the end and the side of the boat together at the same time, being careful not to stitch through the back layer. Make sure that the bottom corner of the boat's front side doesn't hang down below the end – hold it in place with a few stitches. Sew the right-hand edge of the back of the boat to the back side – this will create a good three-dimensional shape.

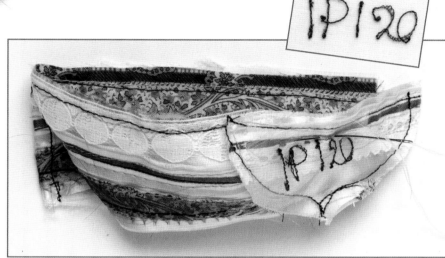

18 Use template Q to create an organza shadow for the boat. Stitch the boat in position on the background, overlapping its shadow, taking care to keep the shape as three-dimensional as possible. Using the templates provided, cut out cotton and organza shapes to create three buoys – place the organza on top of the cotton and machine them in place as shown – sew several times around the inside of each shape. Create a rope for the boat from a thin strip of organza and sew this in place. Embroider a few seagulls in the sky (see page 45), and your piece is ready for mounting.

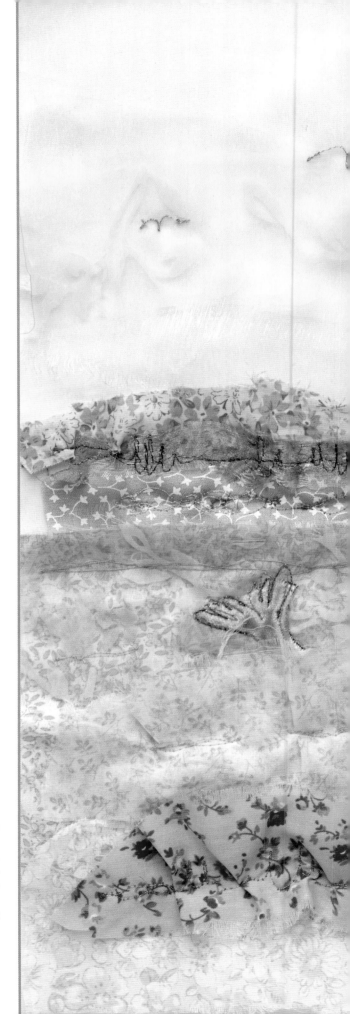

Harbour Scene
40 x 40cm (16 x 16in)
Coastal-themed pictures work so well with my style of embroidery. Building up layers of fabric is a little like building up layers of watercolour. It is a great chance to experiment with fabric patterns to recreate sand dunes and the sea, with quirky features like the seal bobbing along in the harbour.

Templates

The templates given on pages 118–127 are given at actual size unless stated otherwise.

Cupcake Café

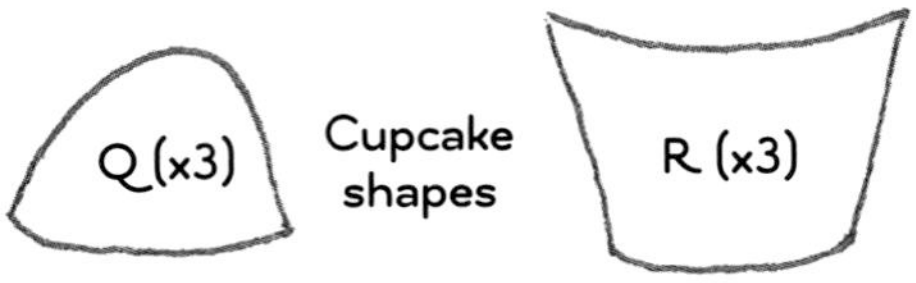

Q (x3)

Cupcake shapes

R (x3)

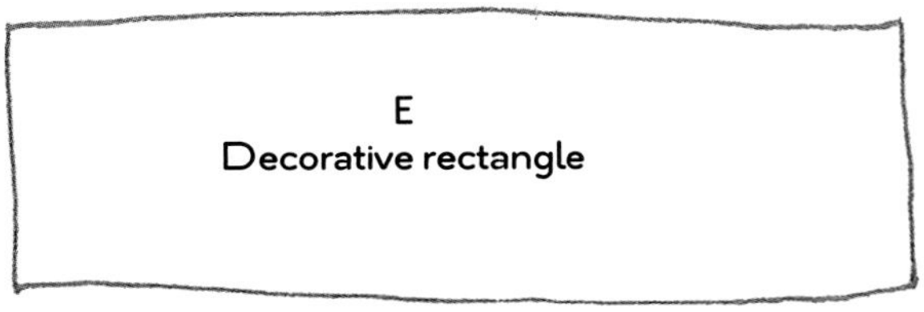

E
Decorative rectangle

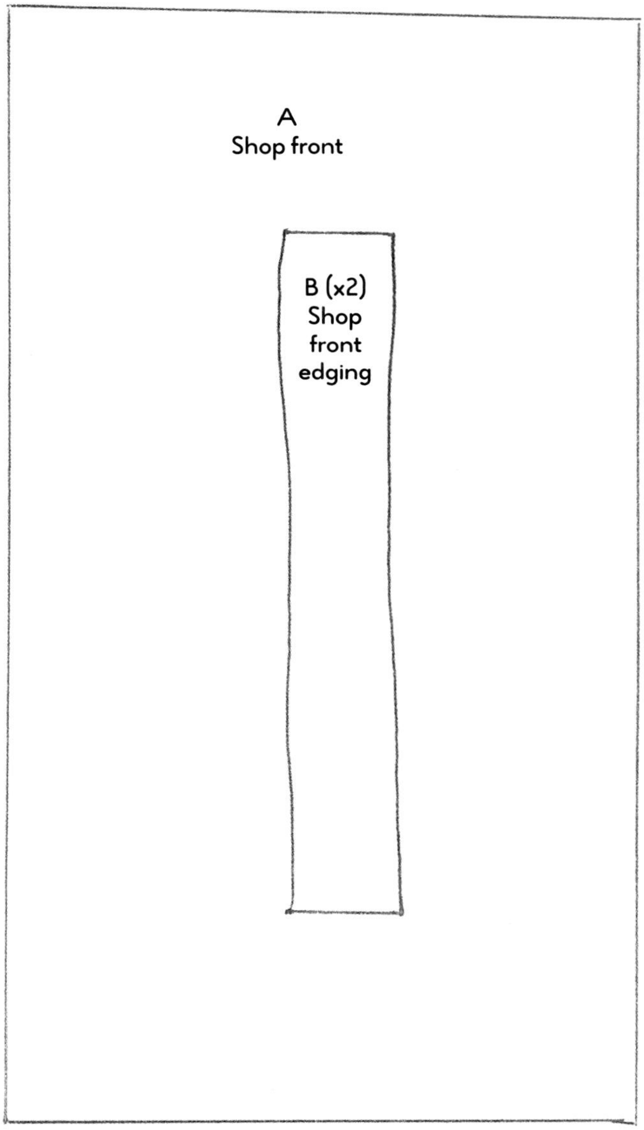

A
Shop front

B (x2)
Shop front edging

C (x2)
Pavement and foreground
Shown here at 50 per cent

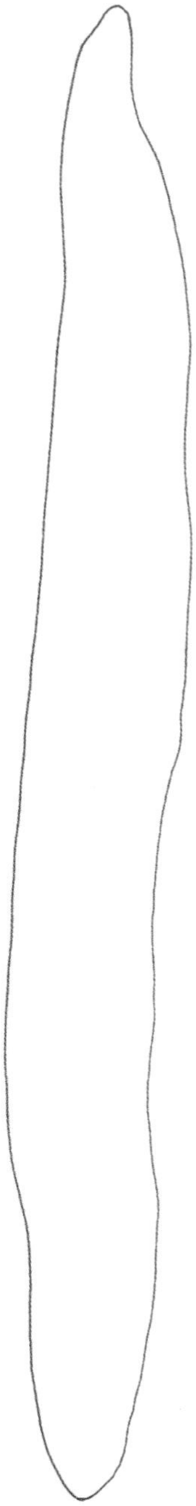

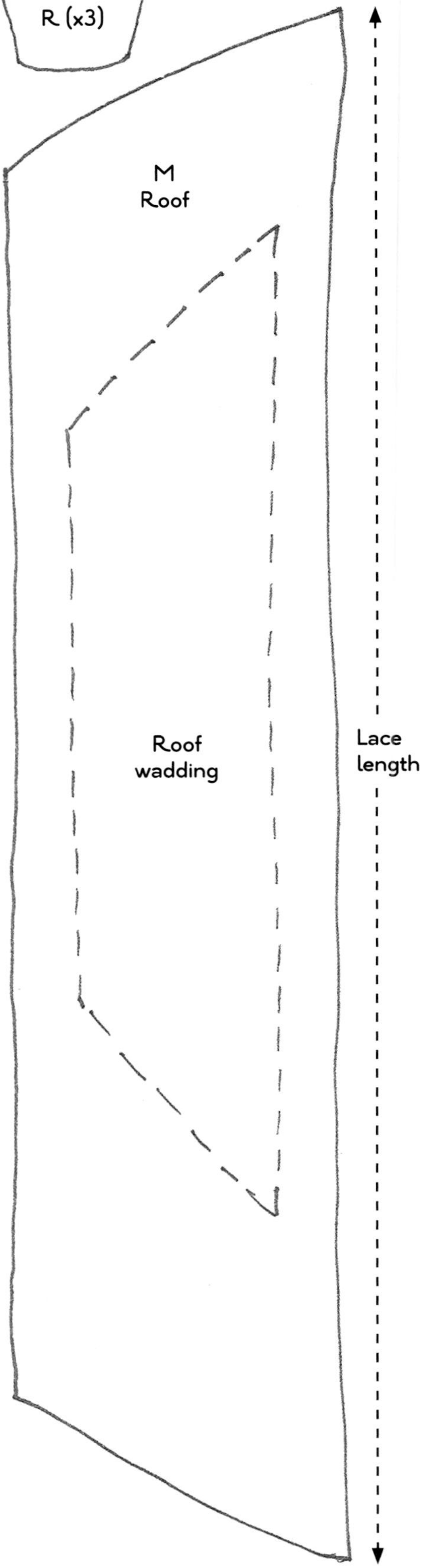

M
Roof

Roof wadding

Lace length

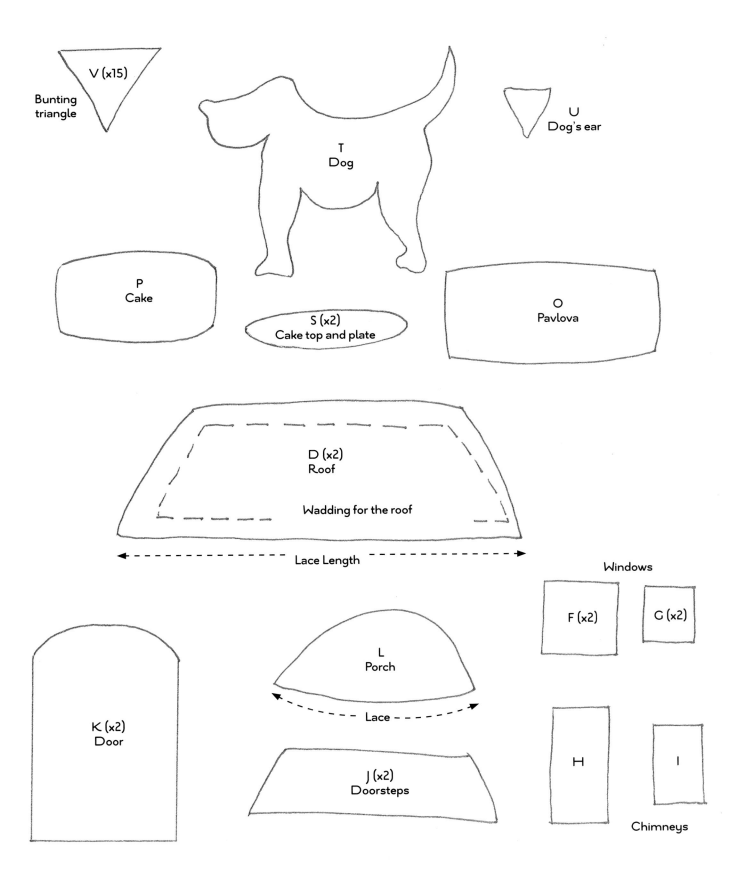

V (x15)
Bunting triangle

T Dog

U Dog's ear

P Cake

S (x2) Cake top and plate

O Pavlova

D (x2) Roof

Wadding for the roof

Lace Length

Windows

F (x2)

G (x2)

K (x2) Door

L Porch

Lace

J (x2) Doorsteps

H

I

Chimneys

Cakestand and Sugar Bowl

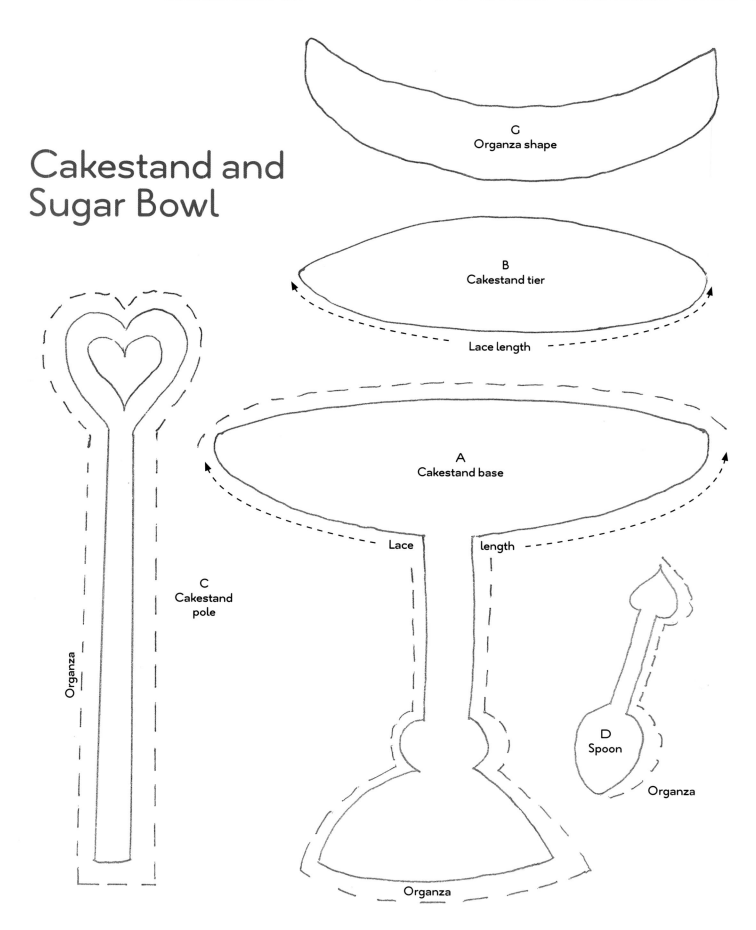

G
Organza shape

B
Cakestand tier

Lace length

A
Cakestand base

Lace   length

C
Cakestand
pole

Organza

D
Spoon

Organza

Organza

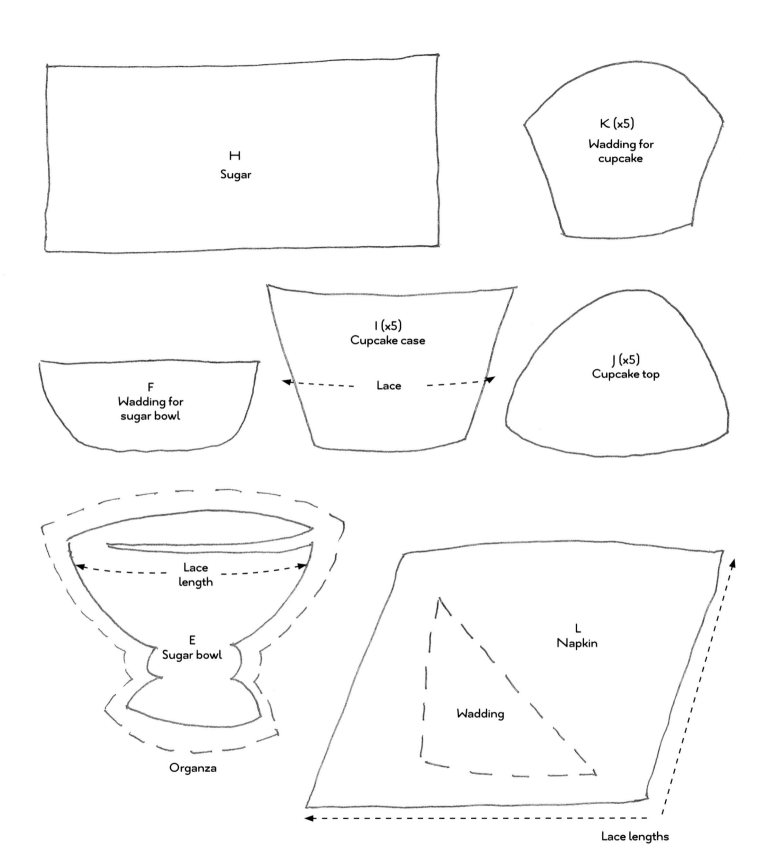

H
Sugar

K (x5)
Wadding for
cupcake

I (x5)
Cupcake case

Lace

J (x5)
Cupcake top

F
Wadding for
sugar bowl

Lace
length

E
Sugar bowl

Organza

L
Napkin

Wadding

Lace lengths

Cottage Garden

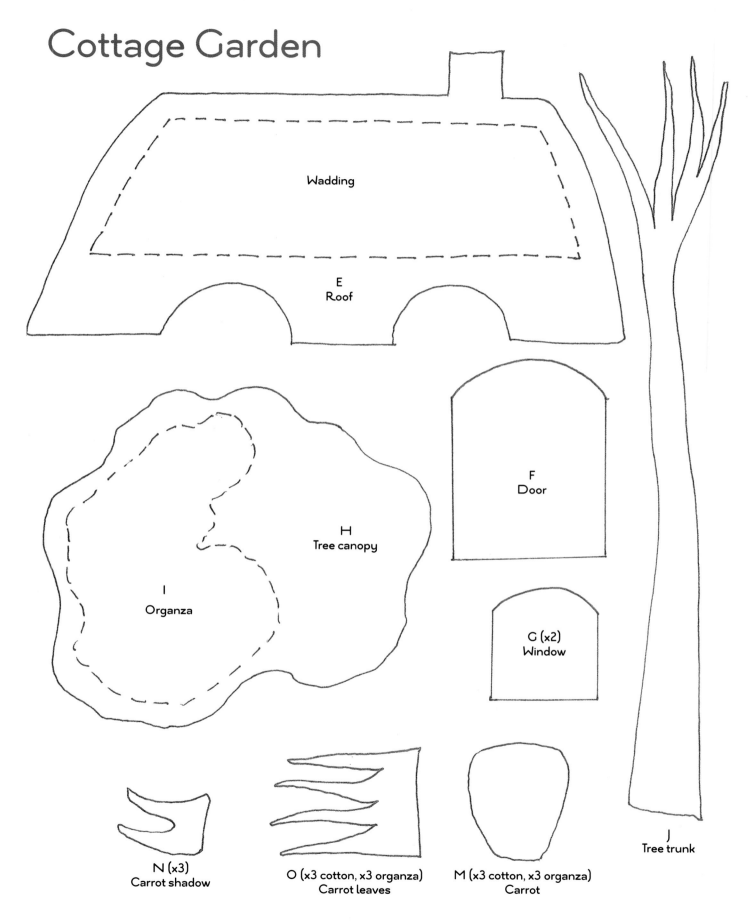

Wadding

E
Roof

H
Tree canopy

I
Organza

F
Door

G (x2)
Window

J
Tree trunk

N (x3)
Carrot shadow

O (x3 cotton, x3 organza)
Carrot leaves

M (x3 cotton, x3 organza)
Carrot

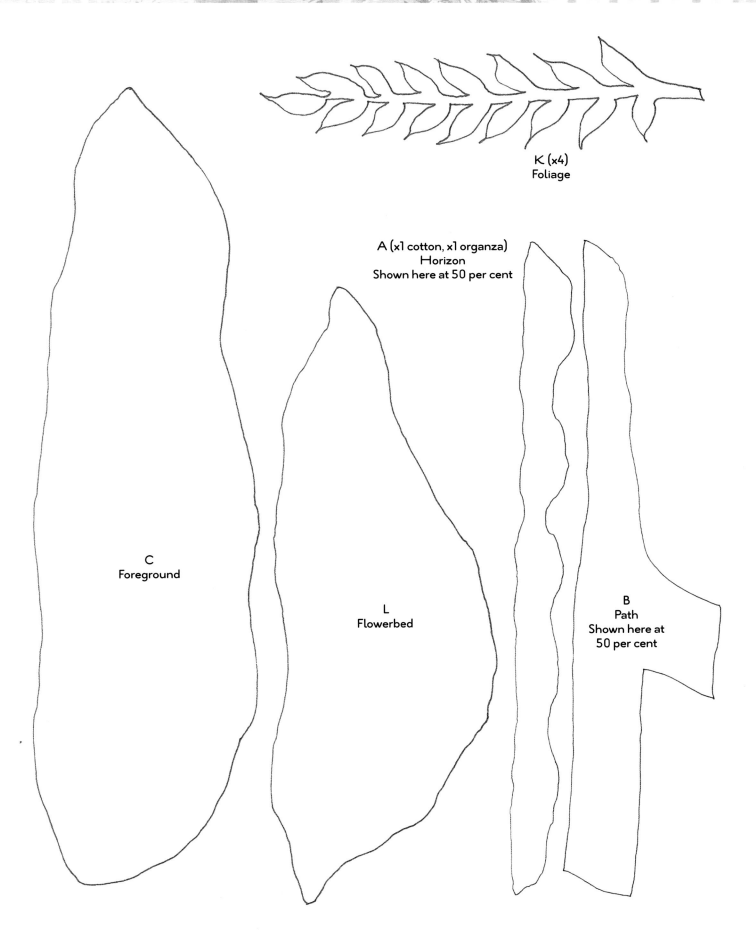

K (x4)
Foliage

A (x1 cotton, x1 organza)
Horizon
Shown here at 50 per cent

C
Foreground

L
Flowerbed

B
Path
Shown here at
50 per cent

Hen House

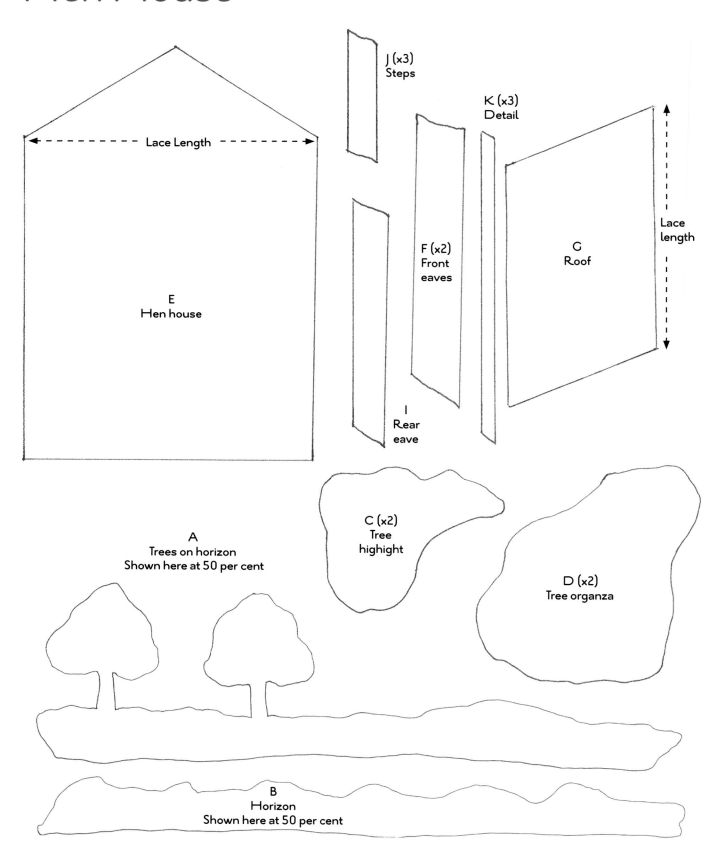

J (x3)
Steps

K (x3)
Detail

Lace Length

F (x2)
Front
eaves

G
Roof

Lace length

E
Hen house

I
Rear
eave

C (x2)
Tree
highight

A
Trees on horizon
Shown here at 50 per cent

D (x2)
Tree organza

B
Horizon
Shown here at 50 per cent

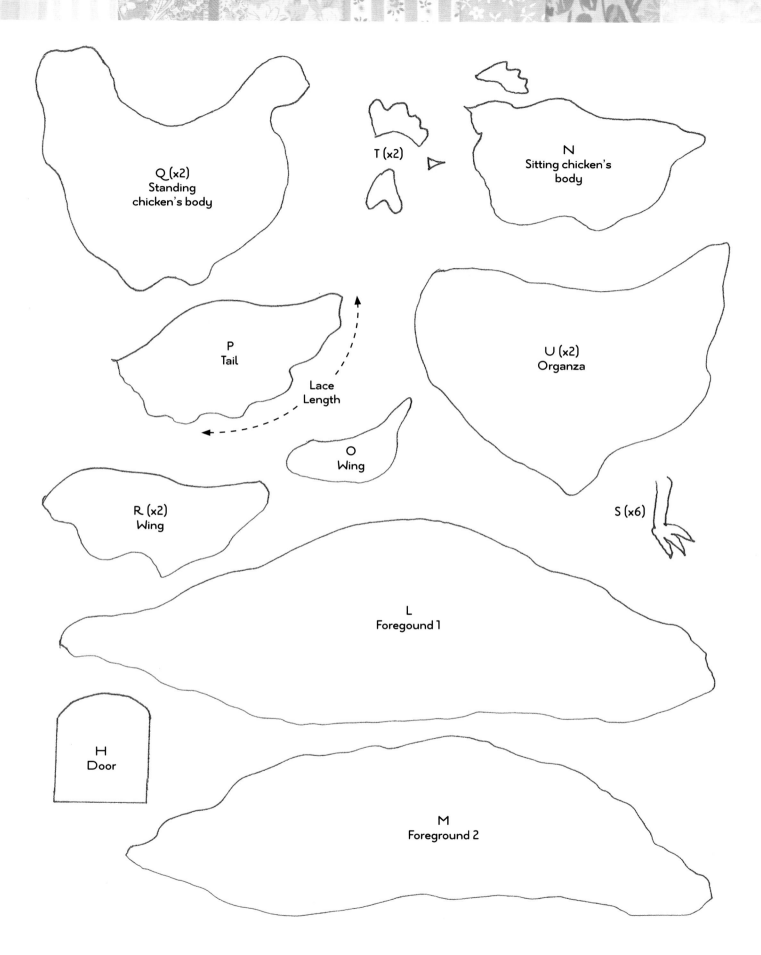

Q (x2)
Standing
chicken's body

T (x2)

N
Sitting chicken's
body

P
Tail

Lace
Length

∪ (x2)
Organza

O
Wing

R (x2)
Wing

S (x6)

L
Foreground 1

H
Door

M
Foreground 2

Harbour Scene

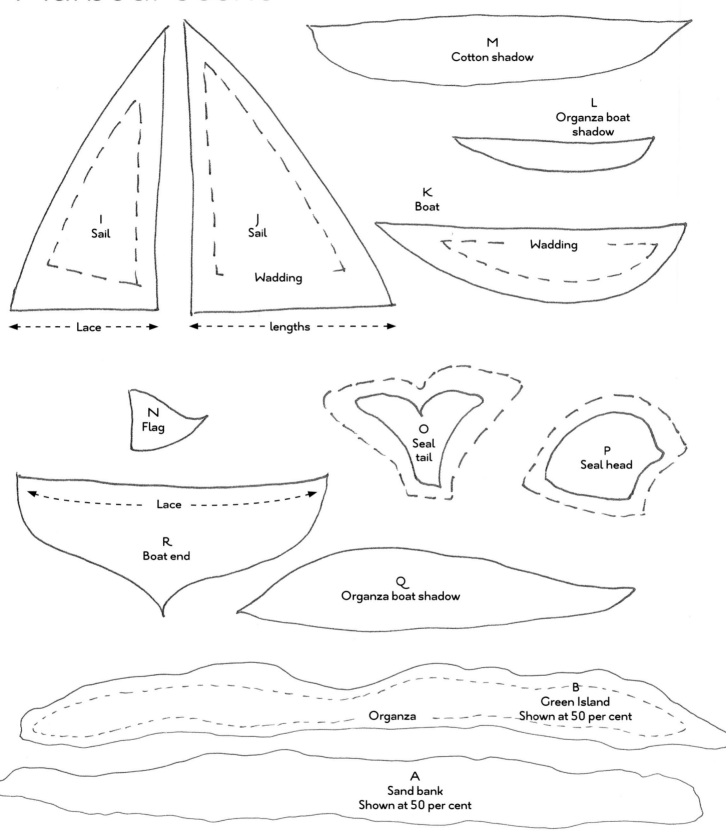

M
Cotton shadow

L
Organza boat
shadow

I
Sail

J
Sail

Wadding

K
Boat

Wadding

← – – – Lace – – – →   ← – – – lengths – – – →

N
Flag

O
Seal
tail

P
Seal head

← – – – – – Lace – – – – – →

R
Boat end

Q
Organza boat shadow

Organza

B
Green Island
Shown at 50 per cent

A
Sand bank
Shown at 50 per cent

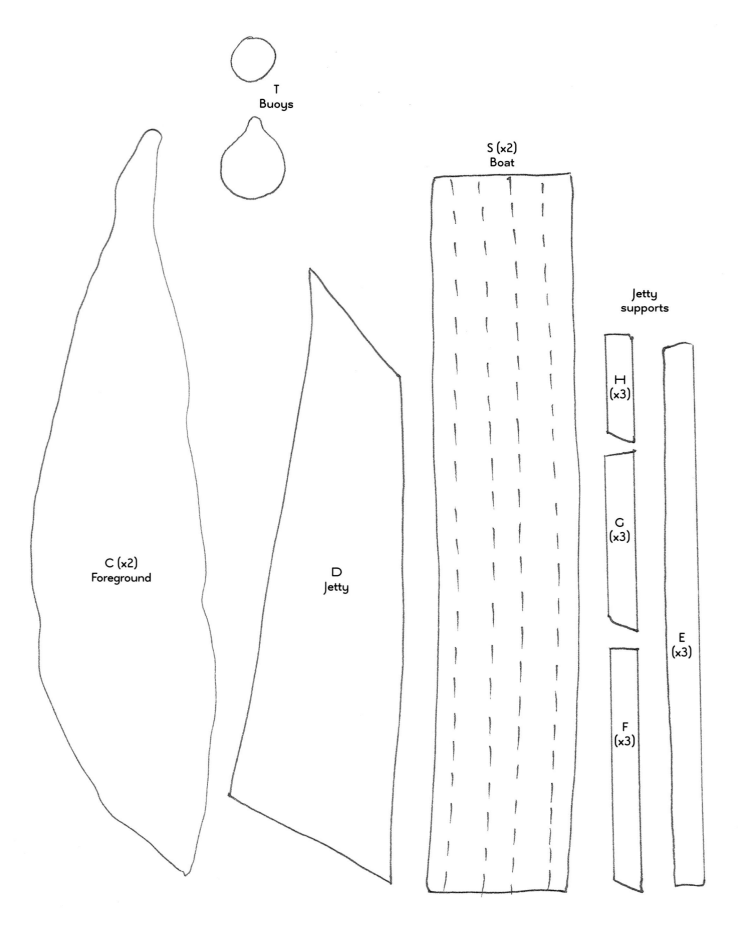

T
Buoys

S (x2)
Boat

Jetty
supports

H
(x3)

C (x2)
Foreground

D
Jetty

G
(x3)

E
(x3)

F
(x3)